IT'S YOUR CALL!

IT'S YOUR CALL!

BASEBALL'S ODDEST PLAYS

THE EDITORIAL STAFF OF BASEBALL AMERICA

Collier Books • Macmillan Publishing Company
New York
Collier Macmillan Publishers
London

TO THE UMPIRES, BASEBALL'S UNSUNG HEROES

Collier Books
Macmillan Publishing Company
866 Third Avenue, New York, NY 10022
Collier Macmillan Canada, Inc.

Library of Congress Cataloging-in-Publication Data
It's your call!
1. Baseball—United States—Umpiring.   I. Baseball
America.
GV876.I86   1989   796.357'3'0973   88-36217
ISBN 0-02-028141-2

Macmillan books are available at special discounts for
bulk purchases for sales promotions, premiums,
fund-raising, or educational use. For details, contact:

Special Sales Director
Macmillan Publishing Company
866 Third Avenue
New York, NY 10022

10 9 8 7 6 5 4 3 2 1

PRINTED IN THE UNITED STATES OF AMERICA

CONTENTS

Acknowledgments, vii

Foreword by Harry Wendelstedt, ix

Introduction, xi

PART ONE: HISTORICAL HYSTERIA
Twenty True Tales That Will Shock and Amaze, 1

PART TWO: TRUE CONFESSIONS
Real-Life Stories from Professional Umpires, 21

PART THREE: HYPOTHETICAL HORRORS
Ninety Questions That Will Test Your Knowledge
of the Rules, 65

ACKNOWLEDGMENTS

Baseball America would like to thank veteran National League umpire Harry Wendelstedt for providing guidance for this project. We would also like to thank American Association umpire Charlie Reliford for helping on the rules interpretations and for his advice.

Thanks also are due to all the other umpires who regaled us with the wildest and wackiest stories they could remember: Greg Bonin, Rick Darby, Gerry Davis, Dana DeMuth, Brian Gorman, Angel Hernandez, Jerry Layne, Ron Luciano, Tony Maners, Randy Marsh, Jack Oujo, Pam Postema, Scott Potter, Dutch Rennert, Vic Travis and Al Somers.

Writer Randy Rorrer would like to thank his father, Louisville sportswriter and noted author George Rorrer, who helped line up interviews with some of the American Association umpires. Randy also would like to express his gratitude to his wife, Kelle, whose patience and support were appreciated.

Editor Jon Scher would like to thank Rick Wolff of Macmillan Publishing, for developing the concept that became *It's Your Call! Baseball's Oddest Plays*. Jon also is grateful to the inventors of the word processor and the electronic spell checker, for making it possible to tackle a project like this during the craziness of a typical summer at *Baseball America*.

FOREWORD

 The job of a professional baseball umpire is one that is exciting, challenging and very difficult. But most fans don't realize this. Most fans feel they could do better than the umpire.

But the umpire must make instant judgments —and he must be correct in his judgments or he won't be employed long. His knowledge of the rules must be complete, and he must act with complete impartiality in reaching fair decisions.

Still, the umpire is a person who fans, players, managers love to hate. Little thought is ever given to the umpire: his feelings, his background and experiences and how dedicated he must be to become good at his job.

Second-guessing the umpire is the American way. It has become a national pastime on its own.

In *It's Your Call! Baseball's Oddest Plays,* *Baseball America* correspondent Randy Rorrer and editor Jon Scher give you an opportunity to test your knowledge of the game, share real-life experiences of umpires and have a taste of some real inside baseball.

As a true baseball fan, you will relish this opportunity to share and compare baseball knowledge with some of baseball's finest officials. You will laugh at some of the strange things that have happened to many of us, and you will gain an insight to this game you never had before.

This is an experience I'm sure you will enjoy.

Harry Wendelstedt
National League Umpire

INTRODUCTION

 An umpire is supposed to be perfect when he accepts the job, and should improve from there. Right?

That's what most fans think, anyway. And that's what aspiring umps are told when they attend schools designed to prepare them for a professional career.

But, like a sharp grounder hit on a poorly kept field, things don't always go as expected. And the umpire who is able to think quickly on his feet, much like the infielder who is able to react quickly and correctly under adverse conditions, is the one who eventually makes it to the big leagues.

In this book, *Baseball America* correspondent Randy Rorrer and associate editor Jon Scher illustrate the many unusual situations that can confront an umpire—and test your knowledge of the rules. First we examine some of the strangest situations that have confronted umpires in the history of the game; second we describe the real-life experiences of professional umpires; and finally we present you, the reader, with tough hypothetical situations.

Throughout the book, we'll let you make the call.

There's even a promotion chart at the back of the book. You can grade your umpiring expertise. Do you belong in rookie ball, the La-Z Boy League or the Hall of Fame?

Turn the page and find out.

PART ONE
HISTORICAL HYSTERIA

TWENTY TRUE TALES
THAT WILL SHOCK AND AMAZE

 Ballplayers are long remembered for extraordinary feats on the playing fields. Who can forget the sixty-one-homer season of Roger Maris, or Joe DiMaggio's fifty-six-game hitting streak?

Umpires, however, are seldom remembered for positive reasons. Good calls on close plays are to be expected. If an umpire makes the correct ruling on a bizarre situation it is because he should know the rules. But, when an umpire misses a close call, the wrath of the baseball world can come tumbling down on him. Think about poor Don Denkinger, the umpire whose call of "safe" on a close play at first base contributed to the Kansas City Royals' come-from-behind victory in Game Six of the 1985 World Series. When TV replays cast doubt on Denkinger's call, he was excoriated by players, managers and fans.

In this section of *It's Your Call!* we'll take a closer look at some of the more unusual plays in baseball history. You may remember the most recent situations. Others were collected by researching musty old baseball books tucked away in the dark recesses of libraries.

These are the calls that tried the souls of umpires throughout the land.

I: THIS SPUD'S FOR YOU

Dave Bresnahan decided the Williamsport Bills needed a shot in the arm during a 1987 Eastern League game against Reading.

And when Bresnahan, a catcher with a .149 batting average, fired a peeled potato into left field in an attempt to deceive a runner, it afforded home plate umpire Scott Potter a chance to make an unusual rule interpretation.

Bresnahan became a mash hit. Many thought the call was rotten. And the decision certainly will be hashed over for years to come.

Seventh-place Williamsport was playing third-place Reading in a meaningless late-season game when Bresnahan executed his plan. It involved a peeled potato, which he had hidden in his back pocket, and a runner on third base. Bresnahan faked a pickoff attempt to third, firing the potato wildly into the outfield.

When Reading runner Rick Lundblade bolted home on the apparent error, Bresnahan tagged Lundblade out with the original ball. The turn of events surprised both Lundblade and umpire Potter.

Is the runner out, safe, or is it a dead ball and no play? Do you eject Bresnahan for making a mockery of the game?

It's your call.

POTTER CALLED LUNDBLADE SAFE. He chastised Bresnahan for pulling the prank, although the catcher was allowed to remain in the game. Williamsport manager Orlando Gomez fined Bresnahan $50. The penalty was stiffened by the Cleveland Indians, the Bills' parent club, who released the light-hitting catcher.

Bresnahan gained national attention with the stunt, and paid his fine by dumping fifty potatoes on the manager's desk along with a note: "Orlando, this spud's for you."

Later, the Bills held a promotion at the ballpark, letting fans use potatoes as tickets. Bresnahan even earned a guest spot on the "Late Night With David Letterman" television show.

"Geez, Steve Howe got five chances to play this game after using drugs," Bresnahan said. "I was just trying to have some fun playing minor league baseball. We were twenty-seven games out. Reading was already in the playoffs. I just figured, 'What the hell.'"

2: THE PINE TAR RAG

Psst. Have you heard the one about the pine tar rag, George Brett and Billy Martin? You probably have, but we're going to tell it anyway. It's an incredible story.

The participants: Kansas City Royals third baseman George Brett, New York Yankees manager Billy Martin and American League umpire Tim McClelland. Oh yeah, and a sticky pine tar rag, the kind players wipe on their bats to improve their grip.

Brett was on one of his typical hot streaks. On June 24, 1983, he blasted an apparent two-out, two-run homer off Yankees ace reliever

Rich "Goose" Gossage to put the Royals ahead of the Yankees 5–4 in the top of the ninth inning.

But Martin noticed Brett's bat had pine tar covering more of the handle than the rules allowed. Ever the guardian of the game's integrity, Martin protested to umpire McClelland.

McClelland measured the bat against the width of the plate and discovered that Brett's bat did indeed have pine tar higher on the barrel than the legal limit of eighteen inches.

What would you have done if you were the home plate umpire? Call Brett out for using an illegal bat? Or rule that it had no effect on the home run and allow the two-run dinger to stand?

It's your call.

IN AN AMAZING DEVELOPMENT, possibly for the only time in his checkered career, an umpire agreed with the feisty Martin. McClelland ruled the pine tar was too high, the bat was an illegal bat and, therefore, Brett should be ruled out on the play.

Instead of a home run and the lead, the Royals were out in the ninth and out for the count with the loss.

Needless to say, the Kansas City players and their manager Dick Howser did not stand still for this. Brett charged McClelland and was involved in a memorable shouting match. Howser also argued vehemently and protested the game to the American League office and league president Lee MacPhail.

MacPhail later upheld the protest, overturning McClelland's decision. MacPhail said the interpretation was not within the spirit of the rules. The home run was allowed to stand and the game later was resumed from that point.

The Royals eventually triumphed 5–4, but not before they had made headlines across the country for several days for the bizarre manner in which they had earned the victory.

3: MERKLE'S BONER

On September 24, 1908, the New York Giants and Chicago Cubs were battling for the National League pennant.

The score was tied 1–1 in the bottom of the ninth inning. The Giants had Moose McCormick on third and Fred Merkle on first with two outs.

New York's Al Bridwell lined a hit to center field and McCormick sped home with the apparent winning run. But, in a practice that was common at the time, the nineteen-year-old Merkle stopped short of second base when he saw McCormick cross the plate.

Merkle started toward the clubhouse. Meanwhile, Cubs first baseman Frank Chance saw his chance to save the game. Chance screamed for the outfielders to throw him the ball so he could touch second base and record the force out that would send the game into extra innings.

Giants pitcher "Iron Man" Joe McGinnity realized what Chance was trying to do. McGinnity took it upon himself to try and stop the first baseman. Before Chance could reach the second base bag, McGinnity rushed off the bench and made a flying tackle. By now, jubilant fans had begun to pour onto the field as they made their way toward the exits. McGinnity grabbed the ball from Chance and threw it into the mob.

Chance appealed to umpire Hank O'Day. Had you been O'Day what would you have done?

It's your call.

O'DAY RULED MERKLE OUT because of the interference from McGinnity, and the game ended in a tie. The contest was replayed at the end of the season when the two teams finished in a dead heat for first with records of 98–55.

The Cubs won the replay. Young Merkle had cost his team the pennant, and was dogged for the rest of his life by the memory of "Merkle's Boner."

4: TWO BALLS IN PLAY

Here's a wild one. Stan Musial of the Cardinals is hitting on June 30, 1959, when Chicago Cubs pitcher Bob Anderson delivers his 3–1 pitch. Umpire Vic Delmore calls "ball four," but catcher Sammy Taylor argues Musial tipped the ball foul and the count should be three and two.

Meanwhile the ball has rolled to the backstop and Musial has made his way to first on the base on balls. Taylor continues to argue the call and Musial decides to take off for second base. Chicago third baseman Alvin Dark races in and picks up the ball at the screen and throws it to shortstop Ernie Banks at second base. At the same time, Anderson, who was given a new ball amidst the confusion of the argument, throws the ball he was given to second base.

Anderson's throw was wild and sailed into center field. Musial decided to try for third on the overthrow and Banks tagged him out with the ball he had via the throw from Dark.

What now? You've got two balls in play.

It's your call.

BASE UMPIRE BILL JACKOWSKI ruled Musial out because he was tagged with the original ball. The infuriated Cardinals played the game under protest, but dropped the protest when they went on to win the game 4–1.

5: ANOTHER TWO-BALL CALL

On the next-to-last day of the 1985 season, the Richmond Braves and Tidewater Tides were battling for a playoff spot in the Triple-A International League.

In the fourth inning of this crucial game the Tides had Billy Beane at the plate with a full count. Beane asked for time and stepped out of the batter's box, but home plate umpire Dan Deshaies did not acknowledge Beane's request for the time out.

Richmond pitcher Tony Brizzolara was uncertain whether time had been called or not and he threw wildly to the plate as he tried to stop his motion.

Since the umpire didn't call time, the pitch became ball four. Beane took off for first base, and when Richmond cather Larry "Buck" Owen did not retrieve the ball from the backstop Beane continued toward second.

Meanwhile, Deshaies had provided Brizzolara with a new ball. Imagine Beane's surprise when Brizzolara threw that ball to second to nail him in time.

That's not all. Owen finally chased down the original ball, and his throw to second hit base umpire Larry Reveal and rolled toward right field.

Do you call Beane out at second, or safe at second, or send him back to first base? Or do you call Hollywood and try to sell the rights to the baseball version of the Keystone Kops?

It's your call.

BEANE WAS INITIALLY called out at second, then sent back to first, and then called out again when Richmond manager Roy Majtyka got involved in the argument.

Tidewater manager Bob Schaefer protested the game, won by the R-Braves 1–0 in 11 innings. The protest was disallowed by IL president Harold Cooper. Cooper did, however, release Deshaies as an umpire.

6: YOU'RE GETTING WARMER

In 1911, in an attempt to speed up games, the American League experimented with a rule that forbade pitchers from making warmup pitches between innings.

During a game between the Boston Red Sox and the Philadelphia Athletics, Boston pitcher Ed Karger was sneaking in a few warmup pitches while his teammates were sauntering out to their positions.

Athletics infielder Stuffy McInnis did some sneaking of his own. He jumped into the batter's box and smashed one of Karger's warmup offerings over the outfielders' heads. McInnis rounded the bases with an apparent home run.

Would you have allowed the homer or called no pitch because the ball was not in play?

It's your call.

THE UMPIRES RULED the play was perfectly legal under the rules at that time. Philadelphia was one run richer as Karger's warmup pitch became a gopher ball.

7: LOST IN A FOG

Umpire Frank Dascoli had to employ an unusual method for calling off a 1958 game between the Chicago Cubs and the Milwaukee Braves at Milwaukee's County Stadium.

A fog rolled in during the bottom of the fifth and the Cubs outfielders were mostly hidden from view. Dascoli took his crew into the outfield and had Frank Thomas of the Cubs hit a fungo fly ball. None of the seven men stationed in the outfield could see the ball and the game was declared fogged out.

The men of Wrigley lost a game to even more unusual circumstances in 1946. The Cubs were playing the Brooklyn Dodgers at Ebbets Field when a swarm of gnats descended. It was a sunny day, but the fans were so annoyed at the gnats they waved their white scorecards to shoo them away. The fluttering backdrop impaired the players' ability to see the ball and created a hazard by the sixth inning.

Should games be suspended under these circumstances, or should they be treated like rainouts?

It's your call.

BOTH THE FOGOUT and the bugout were treated the same as a rainout. The Cubs' game against the Braves was canceled since the score was tied and the game had not been played through five complete innings. The bugout reverted back to the last completed inning and the Dodgers were credited with a 2–0 victory.

8: GET OUT OF THE WAY!

What happens when an unstoppable force hits an immovable object?

When Don Drysdale was working on his former major league record of fifty-eight consecutive shutout innings, he nearly lost the string at thirty-six when the Dodgers were playing the San Francisco Giants in May of 1968.

Drysdale loaded the bases with no outs in the eighth inning and was pitching to Giants' catcher Dick Dietz.

With the count at 2–2, Drysdale ran a fastball inside and it hit Dietz on the elbow. The only problem was that Dietz didn't seem to make an effort to move out of the way of the pitch.

Would you award Dietz the base and the Giants the run or simply call the pitch a ball and make the count 3–2?

It's your call.

PLATE UMPIRE HARRY WENDELSTEDT called it ball three. Drysdale went on to get Dietz to pop up, and pitched out of the inning without allowing a run.

"That particular year the Dodgers and Giants were scrapping for the pennant," Wendelstedt said. "I was a fresh young umpire. I was working on a crew for the very crucial series and Drysdale had already pitched four consecutive shutouts. As an umpire you don't care about those things. You see it in the newspaper, but that's not what you're concentrating on. You're concentrating on the next pitch and the next play.

"When I said, 'You're not going to first base,' a half-hour war erupted. I got to run Herman Franks [the manager], I got to run the coach, I got to run a pitcher. I mean it was an absolute war. Here I am in my second year in the major leagues. This is the kind of call that doesn't come from thinking about something, it comes from your gut. It comes from your heart. You realize the basis for good umpiring is common sense and fair play. Here I saw a guy trying to take advantage of the rules and I jumped right on it and wouldn't let him take the base.

"That call was actually the making of me. It really set my name out as an umpire who would do something that he felt was right. It really went a long way in building a reputation for me."

9: REMEMBER ED ARMBRISTER?

When a controversial call occurs in the middle of a pennant race or during the playoffs it gets magnified. When one occurs during a World Series game, it gets blown up to epic proportions.

Just ask Larry Barnett.

The classic 1975 series between the Cincinnati Reds and the Boston Red Sox was tied 1–1 and the third game was knotted 5–5 in extra innings. Cincinnati, the home team, called on pinch-hitter Ed Armbrister to move up Cesar Geronimo with a sacrifice bunt. Geronimo had led off the inning with a single.

Armbrister's bunt was a poor one and it took a high bounce in front of the plate. As Boston catcher Carlton Fisk attempted to come across the plate to catch the ball and throw to second for a force out on Geronimo, he collided with Armbrister, who was trying to make his way to first.

Fisk desperately tried to free himself from Armbrister and finally he leapt and tried to fire the ball to second. Fisk's throw was off target and sailed into center field, allowing the runners to advance to second and third base with no outs.

Would you rule interference or let the play stand?

It's your call.

HOME PLATE UMPIRE BARNETT ruled that there was no interference since Armbrister did not collide with Fisk intentionally. Cincinnati second baseman Joe Morgan followed the arguments with a single to center to score Geronimo and the Riverfront Stadium fans went home happy. The Reds went on to win the series in seven games.

10: SOMETHING UP HIS SLEEVE

Ever hear of an unintentional hidden ball trick?

In a 1948 game between the Philadelphia Athletics and the Boston Red Sox a player lost a ball—not in the sun, or in the lights, in the crowd or even on a roof. He lost the ball in his own uniform.

Here's how it happened: The Red Sox' Billy Goodman was hitting with Ted Williams on third base. Goodman hit a grounder to Athletics shortstop Eddie Joost.

Joost couldn't handle the grounder and the ball ran up his arm and disappeared down the billowing sleeve of his shirt. Teams didn't wear tight-fitting double-knit uniforms then.

Confused, Joost dropped his glove and began to frantically search for the ball. When he found it he hurriedly tried to unbutton his shirt and, deciding that was too slow, he pulled his shirttail out of his pants and let the ball fall out to the ground.

Goodman reached first easily, but a hysterical Williams remained on third base, laughing.

What would you do? Allow the ball to stay in play under these circumstances or call it a dead ball and award each runner one base?

It's your call.

THE CURRENT RULE calls for the latter decision. But in 1948 there was no such rule. The play stood as it was with Goodman on first and a bemused Williams on third.

11: A LATE SUBSTITUTION

Who's on home?

No, this is not an Abbott and Costello adaptation for a catcher's clinic. Instead, it is the introduction to a bizarre rules interpretation that arose in the late 1800s.

Michael Joseph Kelly, or "King" Kelly as he was more commonly known during his playing days, gave umpires reason for pause during one nineteenth century game.

Kelly, who played both outfield and catcher, was riding the pines when an opposing batter popped the ball up toward his team's bench.

Kelly realized none of his teammates had a chance to catch the ball and quickly decided to insert himself into the lineup.

"Kelly now catching," he shouted as he gave chase to the pop-up. Kelly caught the ball, but the umpire would not allow the out, despite the pleadings from Kelly that the rule book clearly read that substitutions could be made at any time.

Kelly was right—there was no rule forbidding this play.

What would you call? Out or foul ball?

THE UMPIRE AT THIS game stuck by his original decision. A rule was added the following winter limiting substitutions to when the ball was not in play.

12: THE EEPHUS PITCH

Noah had his ark, so Pittsburgh Pirates pitcher Rip Sewell decided he wanted an arc of his own.

In 1941 Sewell, who was recovering from a hunting accident in which he was shot in the foot, unveiled a trick pitch he had been working on. The arcing, blooper pitch became known as the "eephus ball."

Sewell would throw the ball about fifteen feet in the air and watch it drop through the strike zone.

By comparison, in United States Slow-pitch Softball Association play, a pitch is declared illegal if it goes above twelve feet high.

Sewell's pitch baffled hitters and umpires alike. Hitters had trouble timing the pitch, and therefore most couldn't hit it. Umpires had trouble calling it. Some umps even refused to call it a strike when it did cross the plate in the strike zone.

What's your call on the blooper ball? Ball, strike or illegal pitch?

IN 1941, SEWELL'S MANAGER, Frankie Frisch, came up with a way to solve the problem. He asked Hall of Fame umpire Bill Klem, then the National League supervisor of umpires, to watch Sewell throw the pitch. Klem obliged and decided the pitch was legal. He instructed the umpires around the league to call it in games. But even with the trick pitch, Sewell led the league with seventeen losses that year.

13: WRONG-WAY RUNNER

When zany Germany Schaefer was playing during the early 1900s he was often known for stealing the show during a game, but one of his weirdest moments came when he stole a base while playing for the Washington Senators.

Schaefer reached first base with the score tied with two outs in the ninth inning. Teammate Clyde "Deerfoot" Milan was on third.

Schaefer decided to attempt a steal of second base, hoping to draw

a throw from the catcher so Milan could complete the double steal and win the game.

Schaefer bolted for second, but the catcher did not risk a throw and Milan was stuck at third.

Not one to give up easily, Schaefer took off on the next pitch—back to first base.

The catcher was so surprised he did not make a throw to first. Schaefer got set to attempt another double steal.

What's your call? Do you send Schaefer back to second, allow him to stay at first or rule him out for running the bases backward?

It's your call.

AT THE TIME, there was no rule forbidding a steal of first from second. The umpire allowed the play to stand, but a new rule was quickly implemented. Today, a player who runs the bases backward is automatically out.

14: UMPIRES STAY AFLOAT

Rub-a-dub-dub, three umpires on a tub.

This tub, however, was a boat. In 1941, the three umpires scheduled to call a Boston Braves–Brooklyn Dodgers game were fogbound on a boat. They did not arrive in time for the start of the game.

What should be done under these circumstances? What happens if an ump can't get to a game because of fouled travel arrangements? Do you postpone the game until the umpires can be there, or use alternate umps?

It's your call.

LEGENDARY MANAGERS Casey Stengel and Leo "The Lip" Durocher struck a quick agreement, deciding to choose a player from each team to handle the officiating chores.

The Braves' Stengel chose Johnny Cooney to call balls and strikes. The Dodgers' Durocher picked Freddie Fitzsimmons to call the bases.

Cooney and Fitzsimmons handled the first inning without incident. The regular umpiring crew finally showed up before the start of the second inning and took over, amid many catcalls from the fans.

15: THEY REALLY BLEW IT

While umpires may occasionally blow a call, a strange situation occurs when a player decides to blow a ball.

This play comes up more often than you might imagine.

In 1940, it was done by Bert Haas, a third baseman with the International League's Montreal Royals. Lenny Randle of the Seattle Mariners did it in 1981. Kansas City Royals third baseman Kevin Seitzer made highlight films in 1987 by trying it.

What each of these players tried was the breathtaking—or should we say breath-giving—stunt of attempting to blow a slow-rolling grounder into foul territory before it reached third base.

Is this play legal as long as the player does not touch the ball in fair territory, or illegal regardless of whether the ball is touched? And if the player has bad breath, should the ball be removed from the game?

It's your call.

STRANGELY ENOUGH, the Haas play in 1940 was ruled a foul ball, since the opposing Jersey City team did not protest the actions of the third baseman. But league president Frank Shaughnessy followed up with a new rule that did not permit a player to blow a ball foul.

On Randle's play, the ball was initially ruled foul by home plate umpire Larry McCoy, but he quickly changed his call when Kansas City manager Jimmy Frey protested.

Randle, tongue and breath in cheek, denied blowing on the ball after the game. Instead, he said, he used the power of suggestion to guide the ball foul by telling it to roll foul.

16: THE SHOESHINE BOYS

A couple of cans of shoe polish may very well have changed the course of history in separate World Series.

In the 1957 series between the Milwaukee Braves and New York Yankees, the play in question occurred in Game Four, with the Yankees leading the series 2–1. The game was tied 4–4 after nine innings and New York had scored a run in the top of the tenth to take the lead.

Milwaukee pitcher Warren Spahn was due to lead off the bottom of the tenth for the Braves and Vernal "Nippy" Jones was sent in to pinch-hit for the ace righthander.

16

Yankee pitcher Tommy Byrne delivered a low and inside pitch to Jones.

"Ball one," called home plate umpire Augie Donatelli.

Jones began to argue that the pitch hit him on the foot. When the ball was retrieved it seemed to have shoe polish on it.

Is the shoe polish enough evidence to change the call? Or should you tell Jones you have to see the ball hit him?

It's your call.

DONATELLI REASONED THE ball must have hit Jones and sent the pinch hitter to first base.

Jones came around to score and tied the game and Eddie Mathews belted a two-run homer later in the inning to lead the Braves to a 7–5 victory. Milwaukee went on to win the series in seven games.

Oddly enough, the situation repeated itself in the 1969 World Series between the New York Mets and Baltimore Orioles. This time the call went in favor of the boys from the Big Apple.

The Mets led the series 3–1, but were trailing 3–0 in the fifth game when New York left fielder Cleon Jones led off the bottom of the sixth inning. Orioles pitcher Dave McNally came inside with a low curveball and umpire Lou DiMuro called it a ball. Jones began to argue that the ball hit him and Mets manager Gil Hodges proved it by showing DiMuro the shoe polish on the ball.

DiMuro, like Donatelli before him, accepted the evidence as irrefutable and sent Jones to first. McNally then served up a home run to Donn Clendenon to cut the lead to 3–2 and New York went on to take a 5–3 victory and wrap up the world championship.

17: CAUGHT IN THE ACT

When a pitcher is doing well he is often said to have good stuff. But, when is good stuff the result of good scuff?

In 1987 a pair of pitchers, the Minnesota Twins' Joe Niekro and the Philadelphia Phillies' Kevin Gross, both were caught with sandpaper on their bodies.

Niekro was hiding an emery board in his back pocket. Gross had sandpaper attached to his glove.

If you are umpiring and you find such paraphernalia on a pitcher, what should you do? Make the pitcher remove the devices or toss the offender out of the game?

IN BOTH CASES IN 1987 the pitchers were ejected from the game. And, to make matters even worse for them, they were given ten-day suspensions by their league offices.

18: PUT CORK IN IT

While scuffing the ball became a hot subject in 1987, there were also rumors of illegal bats being used by major league players. Some said there were more loaded bats than there were loaded fans on nickel beer night.

A new rule was even instituted in 1987 allowing opposing managers to challenge one bat per game for tampering. If a manager challenged a bat, it would be X-rayed following the game to see if it was loaded with illegal material.

Houston Astros outfielder Billy Hatcher was caught red-handed in one game when his corked bat exploded and sent cork flying everywhere. The cork makes the bat lighter, and supposedly makes balls carry farther.

Would you, as umpire, call Hatcher out and eject him immediately or would you let the play develop and then eject Hatcher?

It's your call.

HATCHER WAS IMMEDIATELY called out and given the thumb for using the corked bat. The National League office gave him a ten-day suspension on top of that punishment.

19: A TINY CONTROVERSY

Not all of the weird calls in baseball history have been big calls.

Take the unusual situation brought on when maverick owner Bill Veeck made headlines by sending a midget to the plate in 1951. This was really a small call.

The owner of the last-place St. Louis Browns, Veeck decided to try something interesting late in the season.

St. Louis was playing Detroit in a doubleheader. In the bottom of the first inning in the second game of the twin-bill, pinch-hitter Eddie Gaedel was substituted for leadoff batter Frank Saucier.

Gaedel, all three-foot-seven of him, strode to the plate with the number $\frac{1}{8}$ on his back. Plate umpire Ed Hurley quickly called time-out and demanded an explanation. Browns manager Zack Taylor just as quickly produced a major league contract with Gaedel's signature on it to prove he was legally a player.

What would you do? Allow Gaedel to hit or eject both Gaedel and the manager for making a mockery of the game?

HURLEY FELT HE HAD no choice but to let Gaedel hit. Tigers pitcher Bob Cain walked him on four pitches.

Veeck said he had warned Gaedel that he would be on the roof of the stadium with a rifle aimed at the midget, and if Gaedel swung at a pitch he would shoot.

After Gaedel drew the base on balls he was removed from the game for a pinch runner.

American League president Will Harridge took care of the problem when he would not allow Gaedel's playing contract, saying Veeck's actions were "detrimental to baseball." Gaedel's major league career was over.

20: BULLISH IN DURHAM

Just when you thought it was safe to go back to the dugout . . .

Here's another bizarre minor league situation, prompted by an alert third base coach:

The world-famous Durham Bulls were playing the Prince William Pirates in a Carolina League game on August 24, 1986.

Durham was batting with one out and a runner, Dave Justice, on second. Boomer Harrison was hitting for the Bulls, who led 5–1.

With two strikes on the batter, Justice attempted to steal third. Prince William relief pitcher David Rooker's offering to the plate bounced in front of the dish, but Harrison still swung at it for strike three.

The Prince William catcher handled the one-hopper and threw Justice out on his attempted steal.

Both teams began to leave the field when Bulls manager Buddy Bailey, coaching at third base, yelled at Harrison to run to first because the catcher hadn't caught the third strike cleanly.

Harrison hadn't stepped in the dugout yet and he raced to first before anybody on the Prince William team realized what was going on.

Harrison didn't stop there. He bolted for second base, and by now, the Pirates knew they better do something. Prince William first baseman Lance Belen got his infield toss-around ball and fired it—to right fielder Todd Smith, who made the tag at second base.

If you're the umpire, what's your call?

HOME PLATE UMPIRE Jerry Meals called Harrison safe at both first and second bases since Prince William did not retire him with the appropriate ball and he hadn't stepped into the dugout before realizing he should run to first base. If Harrison had gone into the dugout, he would have been out.

Harrison advanced to third on a wild pitch, but Prince William got out of the inning without further damage when Rooker got Todd Dewey to ground out to first base.

The Bulls won the game 6–2.

PART TWO
TRUE CONFESSIONS

REAL-LIFE STORIES
FROM PROFESSIONAL UMPIRES

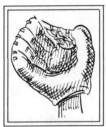Soldiers wounded in action receive the Purple Heart. Perhaps umpires should be given a purple ball-strike counter when they are weirded in action.

Now that we've taken a look through baseball's archives, examining some of the strangest plays in the history of the game, it's time to go to the source: The men and woman who have worn dark blue on fields from Oneonta and Albuquerque to New York and Los Angeles.

The few, the proud . . . the umpires.

In our never-ending quest for baseball's strangest plays and funniest stories, we have interviewed professional arbiters from the lower minor leagues to the majors.

We've spoken with Al Somers, who was involved in baseball as an umpire for thirty-seven years, but never called a regular-season major league game. We've talked with Harry Wendelstedt, the dean of major league umpires in the 1980s. We also heard from Scott Potter, who was the plate umpire in Dave Bresnahan's world-famous spud-tossing play in the Eastern League in 1987, which we related in part 1.

So sit back and enjoy part 2 of *It's Your Call!*, in which we ask our panel of umpires to relate in their own words some of the weirdest situations they ever faced. They'll also tell you about some of the funny things that happened on the way to, and at, the ballpark.

And brace yourself for part 3, in which we will test your umpiring potential with the wildest collection of hypothetical situations ever assembled. The more adventurous readers can skip ahead from time to time.

As always, it's your call.

HARRY WENDELSTEDT

NATIONAL LEAGUE

Born in 1938 in Baltimore, Wendelstedt makes his home in Ormond Beach, Florida. He married Cheryl Maher in 1970 and has two children, Harry III and Amy. Wendelstedt attended Essex Community College and the University of Maryland where he played basketball and baseball. He also played high school and American Legion baseball and professional soccer. He began umpiring in the major leagues in 1966 and had previously umpired in the Georgia-Florida, Northwest, Texas and International leagues. Wendelstedt, who has served four terms as president of the Major League Umpires Association, operates the Harry Wendelstedt School for Umpires in Daytona Beach during the offseason. Wendelstedt spent his free time during the 1988 season writing and fishing.

SINCE THE INFAMOUS pine-tar bat incident in 1983, George Brett and pine tar have often been discussed in the same breath. But Brett should thank Dodgers pitcher Jay Howell, who elevated pine tar controversy to new heights during the 1988 National League Championship Series. Wendelstedt was there, as the left field umpire on a six-man crew working the third game in New York.

Howell came in to pitch late in the game. The trouble began when Mets manager Davey Johnson asked plate umpire Joe West to check Howell's glove.

West called for Wendelstedt, the crew chief, to help him inspect the mitt.

"West took the glove and handed it to me," Wendelstedt said. "The first complaint was about the string. I tried that and I said it looked colored, but there's nothing coming off. Then I opened the glove up and put my hand inside the glove and my hand just stuck there. The entire heel was just covered with pine tar.

"The nonsensical part of the whole thing to me was all the statements made afterward about pine tar not altering the flight of the ball. That's stupid. Who's kidding who? You would have to be an idiot to believe that. If it didn't give him an advantage, why would he be using it? I know guys who can't throw a curveball, but if you give them pine tar they can throw a curveball.

"So that was the situation we wound up with."

Wendelstedt immediately ejected Howell from the game and took the glove over to National League president A. Bartlett Giamatti. After the game, Giamatti issued a three-game suspension to Howell, which was later reduced to two games. The league president also gave the umpires a gag order.

"Giamatti told us he wanted to be the only one making comments on this and asked the rest of us not to do any interviews or say anything, so our hands were tied," said Wendelstedt. "He had a tough decision. It was the first time anybody had ever been banned from the [National League] playoffs. The rule says if a pitcher has pine tar or any foreign substance anywhere on him, he is to be ejected. We did our job and then it was no longer our problem."

ONE OF THE STRANGEST things that ever happened to Wendelstedt had nothing to do with a decision over a strange play. Instead, it involved his decision that the show must go on despite even the most trying conditions.

"I was in my very first game in professional baseball," Wendelstedt recalled. "I had just completed umpire school [Al Somers School for Umpires] in Daytona Beach and I had a job in the Georgia-Florida League. I was assigned to that league and I didn't have a uniform yet, so I ordered it through the mail. The day of the opener my uniform arrived by mail and when I tried it on in the dressing room an hour and a half before game time, my pants fit like leotards.

"During those days I worked with an outside [chest] protector and on the very first pitch of the game I squatted down behind the plate and, rip, there went the seat of my pants. Well the Brunswick [Ga.] newspaper—you know small-town baseball—had a photographer who slipped around behind the screen and took a picture of me down in a crouched position with this big patch of white showing through. The next day on the front of the newspaper was a half-page shot from behind the screen of me back there calling the game. And there was an arrow pointing down to the split in my pants. The headline said, 'Official Opener.'

"That was my start in baseball. That is how I started my career and I figured if I made it through that night after being so humiliated I would be all right. I had no choice because I didn't have another pair of pants."

IT'S FITTING, so to speak, that Wendelstedt got off to an unusual start. His career has been full of the strange and bizarre.

"Weird things happen all the time," Wendelstedt said. "I was behind the plate the night of the famous blackout in the Northeast when New York City and all the surrounding areas lost their lights for three days. We were in about the sixth inning of a ballgame. I squatted down for

the pitch and the pitcher was in the middle of his windup when all of a sudden the lights went, plick, and were out for three days. That was not as funny an experience as driving back into Manhattan that night with no lights on. It was a strange, strange happening."

What's your call when the lights go out?

"It became a suspended game and we resumed it from that point," Wendelstedt said. "When we were able to resume play it was kind of funny because I had a runner on first when all this was going on. And when we were able to resume play we get back on the field and I look and everybody is giggling and the runner is standing on third base. I said, 'No, no, no, we're not starting that. You go back to first base.' "

ONCE WHEN WENDELSTEDT was umpiring the baseball disappeared.

"A pitched ball was thrown in the dirt and there were runners on first and second base," Wendelstedt said. "The ball bounced, caromed off the catcher and went in my ball pocket. Everybody is looking for the ball and nobody knows where the ball is. I didn't know it had gone in my ball pocket. The runners take off and the catcher is yelling 'Where's the ball, where's the ball?' Well it became obvious to me what had happened. I knew that I had two baseballs in my ball bag and now I had three."

What's your call here? Do you tell the catcher where the ball is and get frisked? Or do you halt play and take appropriate action?

"I stopped play and sent the runners back," Wendelstedt said. "I gave the runners one base, which, in my opinion, was what they would have gotten had the ball not gone in my bag. Now there is a rule for that. If the ball lodges in the umpire's or catcher's equipment, it is a dead ball and all runners are awarded one base."

WENDELSTEDT RECALLED another strange play that seemed to interrupt nap time for a couple of players.

"I had a runner on first base and the pitcher balked while trying to pick him off," Wendelstedt said. "I yelled balk at first and I said, 'You, second base,' Well, the pitcher overthrew the ball, and it is still in play on a balk. The runner wasn't paying any attention and he saunters down to second and he's standing there and the ball is laying over by the fence. The game is in Philadelphia and the first baseman was [Pittsburgh's] Richie Hebner. He decided he had better go over and get the ball and he went over and got it and, not realizing the ball was still in play, threw the ball over toward the dugout.

"Now the third-base coach is yelling at the guy on second base to come on over to third, but the guy on second is busy talking to the second baseman and he doesn't hear the coach. With this, the ballboy runs out of the dugout and gets the ball Hebner has thrown in."

What's your call? Do you give the runner an extra base on the interference by the ballboy?

"Well, in a case like this it is a definite case of interference," Wendelstedt said. "But, the intent of the rule is that when there is interference you take such action to eliminate the result of the interference. In other words, I'm not going to let somebody mess up what would have happened. In this case I called time when the interference occurred. They argued that I should award the guy third base. I said absolutely not, if the ball had rolled to the backstop he'd still be talking to the second baseman. He had no idea about advancing. What's kind of amazing about this is that nobody really said anything until later in the inning, so what I ruled is what stood."

RON LUCIANO

AMERICAN LEAGUE, RETIRED

Luciano umpired in the American League from 1968 to 1979. After retiring, Luciano worked as a color commentator on NBC and has written four books based on his career, *The Umpire Strikes Back*, *Strike Two*, *The Fall of the Roman Umpire* and *Remembrance of Swings Past*.

"THE BEST ONE I ever had in my whole life was when the bases were loaded and Toby Harrah was leading off second base. He was playing with Texas at the time, and Billy Martin was the manager," Luciano said.

A ground ball was hit toward Harrah and the shortstop. As Luciano was eyeing the play from the third-base side, he tripped over his size-fifteen feet. Meanwhile, Harrah had managed to get hit by the ball, preventing a possible double play. But Luciano didn't see it.

"Now I look up and I see the ball bouncing back from Toby," Luciano said, laughing.

"The rule is, intentional interference is a double play. You call him out and the batter-runner out. Okay, I've got Billy Martin and I know if I call interference I've got a fifteen-minute argument. If I call double play I've got a thirty- to forty-year argument, at the very least. I never saw it, but I thought, 'Toby, that son-of-a-gun is one of the smartest guys in the world,' so I start screaming, 'Double play, double play, double play!'"

"Toby is standing there and out comes Billy and they're screaming and yelling and I looked at Toby and said, 'Toby, you know and I know you're one of the smartest ballplayers out here. You tell me honestly, you knew that was going to be a double play and you did it on purpose, didn't you?' He said, 'You're right, I am smart.'

"I said, 'Thank you, thank you,' " Luciano said. "It was one of the weirdest things, because I had called a double play that I never saw."

LUCIANO SAID another one of the weirdest plays he encountered in his umpiring career brought about some structural changes at one American League ballpark.

"We're in Cleveland and they have three-inch-wide foul poles," Luciano said. "There's a ball hit down the right field line and I don't know if it's fair or foul. There's eighty-thousand people sitting there and the God's honest truth is, I don't know. I just jumped up in the air because I didn't know and I said foul. It was Cleveland at home and they're out screaming that it was fair and I told them to put up a foul pole."

"Cleveland cannot afford these kind of breaks. So the next day they took a rope and brought it all the way from the bottom to the top [of Cleveland Municipal Stadium]. But what does a rope do in the wind? It blows, and if there's a God in Heaven, I'm there and there's a ball hit down the line and it's obviously, obviously fair. There's no question about it, except the rope blew about three feet in and the ball winds up about three feet on the right side of the pole and the first base umpire screamed, 'Foul, foul, foul!' It was unbelievable."

CHARLIE RELIFORD
AMERICAN ASSOCIATION

Reliford is a thirty-two-year-old umpire from Ashland, Kentucky. He previously umpired in the Appalachian, Florida State and Southern leagues. Reliford, a bachelor, works with his local YMCA, officiates basketball games and works as an instructor for the Harry Wendelstedt School for Umpires during the off-season.

RELIFORD FOUND OUT EARLY in his umpiring career that he would rather fight than switch professions.

"The strangest thing I ever had was when I got in a fight with a manager after the game," said Reliford of an unforgettable night while

he was umpiring in the Florida State League. "It was one of those unfortunate situations that happens in the minor leagues. Sometimes you have to walk off the field with a visiting team. We had had trouble with the [Lakeland] Tigers before and in the sixth inning of this game my partner had to throw the manager [Teddy Brazell] out of the game.

"After the game was over we had to walk up the runway where the manager was. Teddy confronted us on the runway and he and Angel [Hernandez, Reliford's partner] got in a shoving match and when they shoved each other it just exploded and all the players came out on the runway and there were probably twenty guys out there. It was a very unfortunate situation, but nobody really got hurt. There was more pushing and shoving that went on than anything else."

What can an umpire do in a situation like this?

"There's really not much you can do," Reliford said. "You can't throw him out of the game. The game was already over. We reported it to the league office and we had a hearing and one of the surprising things was that the manager of the opposing team [Rick Matthews of the Fort Myers Royals] came over and stood up for us. As it turned out Brazell was suspended for fifteen games and fined $500, which is really steep by minor league standards."

RELIFORD SAID the strangest call he has seen on the field while umpiring occurred while he was working in the Florida State League with Brian Gorman as a partner.

"Fort Myers had runners on first and second and they were going to sacrifice with no outs to move the runners over," Reliford said. "It was a pretty obvious sacrifice situation and everybody was prepared for it. Their batter bunted the ball and the ball went about ten or fifteen feet in the air and about ten or fifteen feet out in front of the plate. The catcher can't find the ball and runs in the wrong direction after it. The pitcher and infielders can't get to the ball. As the infielders and pitcher are coming in the batter inadvertently throws the bat out into fair territory and the ball comes down and hits the bat in fair territory and the ball trickled off the bat into the Fort Myers dugout in dead-ball territory.

"Immediately both managers are out of their dugouts. One is screaming for interference while the other was screaming that his guys should get two bases."

What's your call on the bungled bunt play?

"Gorman had the perfect answer," Reliford said. "He looked at one manager and told him he was right, it was interference, and to get away so he could argue with the other manager. Then he turns around to the other manager and said, 'Look, it's interference, it's one of those crazy plays you've never seen before, but I've had it before and I know what it is.'

"So he convinces the guy that it is interference and that his batter is out since the whole bat interfered with the play. If it had been a splintered bat it would have been nothing. So the batter was out and the runners had to go back to their bases."

RELIFORD ALSO SAID he had to make an interesting call in an American Association game in Denver.

"The pitcher had one of those moves to first base where he usually steps back off the rubber and then over to first," Reliford said. "It is legal, but he becomes an infielder on the play. We had a runner on first base when the pitcher made a quick step back, but when he did he must have changed his mind or had some doubts because he went ahead and delivered the ball to the batter."

"It's a balk, but all the other players were arguing that since he stepped back off the rubber he was an infielder."

What's your call and why?

"Well the rulebook says there are thirteen ways to balk and in those thirteen ways it says 'delivering an illegal pitch,' and if you turn to Rule 2 it says an illegal pitch is (*a*) when a quick pitch or (*b*) when the pitcher delivers the ball to the batter with his foot off the rubber.

"Denver had a hard time accepting that their pitcher could balk when he stepped back off the rubber."

RELIFORD COULDN'T MASK his excitement over a call his crew once made in the Southern League playoffs.

"It was myself, Vic Travis, Joe Mikel and Mike Haley doing the game," Reliford said. "There was a hit right up the middle and the runner on second came around easily to score. The throw comes home from the outfield and the play wasn't even close, so the catcher still has the mask in his hand.

"When the ball hit the edge of the dirt it kind of took a bad hop and the catcher stuck out his mask to catch the ball. So we've got to give the guy on first third base. Being the kind of play you hardly ever see, it started a big argument."

Reliford explained that the penalty for illegal use of equipment on a thrown ball is two bases. The penalty for illegal use of equipment on a batted ball is three bases. (Hint: Watch out for this one in part 3.)

WHEN AN UMPIRE tells a player to hit the showers, it usually means the player has been ejected from the game. During an American Association game in 1988, a player very nearly did hit the showers, literally.

"I was umpiring at third base and the guy hit the ball right over the bag and I pump it fair and go out with the ball," Reliford explained. "In Iowa the dressing rooms are not connected to the dugouts like in many stadiums. Teams have to walk to the left field corner to get to the dressing rooms. As the ball is going down to the left field corner, the ballboy is also walking down to the dressing room. As the ballboy got to the door and opened the door, the action of the door swinging deflected the batted ball past the outfielder and into the left field corner.

"I couldn't believe it. I had never seen anything like that before. We didn't make the call a ground-rule double, but instead we said '9.01c,' which says that anything not specifically covered in the rulebook is up to the umpire's discretion. So we just said we thought he was going to get a triple and it's going to be a triple. It was automatically a triple, we just put him where we think he would have gotten had that not happened.

"Thank God, Rocky Bridges was the manager of the opposing team. He was hilarious. He thought we should have put the runner back at second and we were standing right by third base when he was pleading his case. He pointed at the runner and said, 'Look at this guy, there's no way he could get a triple. He couldn't get a triple when they did deflect the ball.'

"That was just weird. The odds of the kid opening the door at the precise moment the ball got there are phenomenal. The kid never saw the ball. He was a twelve-year-old who had gone in to get some more sunflower seeds and he was really embarrassed and was apologizing. He was about to cry because all these guys were yelling at me and he thought he had caused it."

DANA DEMUTH

NATIONAL LEAGUE

DeMuth, thirty-two, was born in Fremont, Ohio, and now lives in Rancho Cucamonga, California. He worked his first major league game in 1983 and became a regular member of the National League umpiring staff in 1985. He previously umpired in the California, Texas and Pacific Coast leagues and also worked in Colombia and the Dominican Republic during the winter league season. He married Marjorie Whitaker in 1978.

DeMuth recalled his strangest situation—a loaded bat incident in Houston during the 1987 season.

"I was behind the plate and Billy Hatcher was batting," DeMuth said. "I believe there was one runner on and he was on second base. Hatcher hit a ground ball in between third base and shortstop and his bat broke and half the bat went out to third base, [Chicago's] Keith Moreland was playing third base; and the other half was sitting right there at home plate. I was looking at Moreland and Moreland was looking at the bat, one run scored, and then Moreland came running in at me. I picked up the other half of the bat and . . . I could see a groove about seven inches long with cork in it so I knew right away what Moreland was going to complain about.

"About that time John McSherry, the acting crew chief since Billy Williams was out with a broken leg, came in. When something like this happens it's so cut-and-dried that you don't have to go through a lot of real sophisticated stuff to take care of the situation. I kind of got a smile on my face because it was right there—the cork and every-thing—and it is the first time it has ever happened in baseball. I got the other half of the bat from Moreland and showed it to McSherry and said, 'John we've got a problem here,' and John said, 'Dana, wipe the smile off your face, we're on TV.'

"He wanted me out of there because he didn't want me smiling. He said, 'This isn't funny, get outta here.' So we had the corked bat situation, we had to call Billy Hatcher out—throw him out of the game and put the runners back to where they were."

NOT ALL BIZARRE umpiring experiences are quite so humorous, as DeMuth found out while working in the minor leagues.

"I'm from California, and we're used to earthquakes out there," DeMuth said. "I'm in Midland, Texas, one time and San Antonio was in town to play. I was working with another umpire named Jim Johnston. I was behind the plate and we were getting a lot of flak this game because it was a tight game and there were about fifty-mile-per-hour winds. Well I didn't know any better and they said they wanted to start the game and I felt like it was my job to finish it. We go on through the whole game. The ball is blowing all over the place. The dirt is blowing around and getting in the players eyes. They're all crying about wanting to call the game, but I say, 'No, you started it, I'm going to finish it.'

"We finished it. We had two ejections, one from each side. Both managers, because they expressed their thoughts about us playing it too candidly. The game ended and all of a sudden the wind just stopped. So I thought, 'Hey, look at that, I did the right thing after all.'

"We walk off the field and get to our locker room and the clubhouse man runs into the locker room and slams the door and locks it and says, 'Get on the floor!' I said, 'What's going on?' and he said, 'Just get on the floor, we have a tornado coming through.'

"The tornado hit about that time and the door is rattling and rattling and boy was I scared. All of a sudden, the door stopped and things got quiet again. We went outside and looked and the whole screen behind the plate that protects the fans from foul balls and had these aluminum poles, had bent over home plate. If that would have happened fifteen minutes earlier, I wouldn't have known any better and a lot of players and myself could have really been hurt. I'll tell you what, I went to church the next day."

GREG BONIN

NATIONAL LEAGUE

Bonin, thirty-three, was born in Lafayette, Louisiana, in 1955 and still resides there with his wife, the former Judith Norton. The Ragin' Cajun played Colt League and American Legion baseball and is a graduate of Southwestern Louisiana. He began his major league umpiring career in 1984 and became a regular on the National League staff in 1986. He previously umpired in the Florida State, Texas and International leagues, as well as in Colombia and the Dominican Republic during the winter. Bonin enjoys fishing, hunting and golf.

MANY TRADITIONALISTS DISDAIN the high-five greeting and its variations, used by players to congratulate each other. Bonin gives an excellent example of how the high five can be hazardous to the success of a ballclub.

"We were in Chicago with the Phillies in there," said Bonin of a 1987 contest. "We were in the sixth inning and the Phillies were down two runs. Jeff Stone was on second and Juan Samuel was on first. I think it was Von Hayes who hit a double down the third-base line, and both guys came around to score.

"Well, Stone scored and Samuel was coming in to score and Stone turned around to give him the high five and Samuel stepped about a foot in front of the plate and a foot beyond the plate and just kept running right into the dugout.

"[Cubs catcher] Jody Davis hadn't seen it, but I saw it and everybody around the plate is screaming, 'Appeal, appeal, appeal!'

"Davis turns to me and asked if 'he' touched the plate and I asked, 'Which one?' He said Samuel, so I didn't say anything and he decided to appeal."

Davis went to the pitcher and they appealed the play.

"I called Samuel out and nobody could believe that that could happen. But when we looked at the videotape the next day, it wasn't even close. He missed the plate by about a foot on both sides, so I felt vindicated."

TONY MANERS

AMERICAN ASSOCIATION

Maners has umpired in the minor leagues for twelve years. The thirty-five-year-old was born in Indianapolis and now resides in Orlando, Florida, in the off-season with his wife and son. Maners has umpired in the Western Carolinas (now the South Atlantic), Southern, Pacific Coast and International leagues as well as the American Association. Maners attended the Al Somers School for Umpires. He has been an instructor at the Harry Wendelstedt School for Umpires, worked for the YMCA, officiated college and high school basketball games and worked for the College Sports Festival, a national student competition based in Daytona Beach.

MANERS HAS SPENT so much time watching major league prospects and rejects play for farm teams across the nation, he should apply for a subsidy from the U.S. Department of Agriculture. With all that experience, the longest season Maners ever spent was the International League *game* he called between the Pawtucket Red Sox and the Rochester Red Wings, at Pawtucket's McCoy Stadium in 1981. It was the longest game in professional baseball history.

"It was a Saturday night, April 18, before Easter," Maners said. "The game started half an hour late because they had three light poles out. We got one to come back on and the managers agreed to play with the two poles out. So we started the game and in the sixth inning one team scored to make it 1–0 and Pawtucket scored in the bottom of the ninth on a sacrifice fly to tie it. There were about four or five balls hit that night that were possible home runs, but the wind kept bringing them back into the park.

"My two partners [Jack Lietz and Dennis Cregg] had worked a game the year before that went twenty-two innings and tied the record for the longest game in the league. Dennis had moved his family from a third-story apartment building for eight hours that day and almost called in sick because he was so tired. The only reason he probably didn't do it was because our other partner, John Hirschbeck, had just been called up to replace somebody in the major leagues and left us with three guys.

"After about twenty-two or twenty-three innings in this game Jack came over to me and said we might want to start thinking about a curfew here. I said, 'No Jack, being the first year in this league I really went over the interpretation manual and there's nothing in there. It says curfew as imposed by law and unless you know of a curfew in this city, we can play all night.'

"I had it [the manual] memorized and even came in between innings and showed it to him, where it was in the book. In the meantime, the managers and general manager, who had received the same manual, had a different writing on their page sixteen that said curfew at 12:50 A.M. No inning was supposed to start after that. When we got these two books together it was about two in the morning and we saw the discrepancy and Jack, being the crew chief, said he thought we should continue with the game.

"We went on with the game and finally the [Pawtucket] general manager called the league president and woke him up at about a quarter 'til four. The league president called back and called Jack off the field, so we kid around with him saying he should have an asterisk beside his name because he missed two outs.

"When Jack got back he said that Mr. [Harold] Cooper told us to call the game at the end of the next full inning and that was the thirty-second. It was 4:07 in the morning and they were playing 'Daybreak' by Barry Manilow, and Lionel Richie's 'All Night Long.'

The crowd of nearly two thousand had dwindled to about twenty when they called it at 4:07.

"There were drunks stumbling in who had seen the lights on at the field and wanted to see what was going on," Maners said.

"When we came off the field we knew we had set some kind of record. As a kid you memorize a lot of stats off the back of baseball cards and stuff and I had been into the *Guinness Book of World Records* and knew that the longest game in history had been twenty-nine innings, but I didn't know who had done it or what. When we got to the thirtieth I knew we had some kind of record.

"I had gloves on for sixteen innings and Jack's hands were turning blue on him because it was so cold. It was near thirty-eight degrees and the wind chill even made it colder. I let him use the gloves and told him I had them for the first sixteen innings and he could have them for the next sixteen, not knowing that that would be the magic number. That was kind of ironic."

The game was called after thirty-two innings and the two clubs were scheduled to meet the next afternoon for a 2 P.M. game. The clubs decided it would be best to complete the marathon game the next time Rochester came to Pawtucket.

"We went ahead and played the afternoon game and it was tied 3–3 in the ninth inning when a pinch hitter, Sammy Bowen, hit a three-run homer to end it.

"They decided to pick up the game on June 23 and right away we ran into our dressing room to see where we were going to be because we wanted to work it. As luck would have it we were scheduled in for those four days only, our only other trip to Pawtucket the rest of the year."

When June 23 rolled around, McCoy Stadium was jammed. The big crowd got only a brief glimpse of the historic game, however, as Pawtucket rallied for a run in the bottom of the thirty-third inning.

"You had players like Bobby Ojeda in the game, Wade Boggs, Marty Barrett, Rich Gedman, Cal Ripken, Jr., and a few others who have made it to the big leagues," Maners said.

How did the umpires make it through the night?

"The only thing I had all night were two candy bars at about 2:30, which would have been about the twenty-fifth or twenty-sixth inning," Maners said. "The ballplayers had eaten everything in the clubhouse and the concession stands had been closed long before then. Jack still jokes and takes great pride in the fact that we never left the field to go to the rest room. We stood out there the whole eight hours."

WHILE MANERS IS HAPPY to be remembered as one of the umpires in the thirty-three-inning drama, he said he has had days he didn't care to remember.

"Back in A-ball I had a game between Spartanburg and Greenwood," Maners said. "You know how first basemen like to cheat a little bit by pulling off the bag early.

"I had a play where the guy is out by ten, twelve feet and the first baseman comes way off the bag and caught the ball early. I said safe with my voice and out with my arm, because I was thinking at that moment that is going to be an easy out.

"I called time-out right away and headed for the third-base coaching box, because I knew the manager there, Mike Compton, would be coming. I said 'Mike, I've probably done a major sin right here. I called the play a little too quick and I said one thing and I did the other. Everybody in the ballpark saw me motion with the out call and that's what I'm going to stick with.'

"That was probably the worst situation I've been involved with because I knew I actually kicked the play early and had to live with it. It was probably the most embarrassing thing that ever happened to me."

ANGEL HERNANDEZ

AMERICAN ASSOCIATION

Hernandez, twenty-seven, resides in Miami during the off-season with his wife and two daughters. Hernandez previously worked in the Florida State, Carolina, and Southern leagues.

HERNANDEZ DISCOVERED early in his career that a manager's bark is often worse than his bite—especially if the manager is wearing dentures.

"I was in the Carolina League and Bill Slack was the manager for Winston-Salem," Hernandez said. "This lefthander they had used a high step and he always passed the plane to go home and I would consistently balk him.

"So we're calling a game and he passes the pitcher's plane and I call a balk.

"Slack comes out and he's yelling at me and you can hear him all over the stadium. He goes on and on and on and on and then his teeth popped out on him and fell right in the dirt. I don't know how we kept from laughing. John Spange, my partner, turned away and when he did I don't know how I kept from losing it. But we laughed about that the rest of the season and even when he sees me now he'll ask if I remember when Slack lost his teeth and picked them up and put them back in to argue after he had stepped on them."

Hernandez found himself put in a strange position in a game in Louisville in August 1988. In the process, he provided young Troy Billings with an impromptu Spanish lesson.

Van Snider of the Nashville Sounds had hit a grand-slam home run in the top of the ninth inning to give the Sounds an 8–4 lead over Louisville. Redbirds manager Mike Jorgensen came out of his dugout to argue Hernandez's calls on balls and strikes—which earned Jorgensen an automatic ejection from the game.

After the top of the ninth ended, Billings, the batboy, came out to give Hernandez some new baseballs.

What the sixteen-year-old, soft-spoken Billings didn't realize was that the Redbirds' Mark Daugherty had written a pointed message to Hernandez on one of the balls.

After delivering the baseballs and witnessing Hernandez's reaction, Billings began to walk back toward the dugout. The batboy was promptly ejected from the game as well.

"Some of it was in Spanish and I didn't understand what it meant," Billings said of the message. "I know now."

Hernandez knew right away what it meant—and it meant the end of the game for Billings.

Jorgensen spoke on Billings' behalf.

"I've never seen a batboy get thrown out and I'm not sure why it happened," Jorgensen said. "He's about the nicest kid you've ever seen. I expected to get thrown out, I thought he missed a couple of pitches and I thought I needed to say something."

Next, time, better read the fine Spanish print first.

JACK OUJO

AMERICAN ASSOCIATION

Oujo, twenty-nine, has been umpiring for eight years. He began his arbiting career in the New York–Penn League and worked his way up through the South Atlantic and Southern leagues and worked his fourth year in the American Association during 1988. He lives in Freehold, New Jersey, during the off-season.

OUJO HAD TO MAKE a quick ruling on a strange play while he was calling a game in the South Atlantic League.

"There was a runner on second base and the pitch was in the dirt," Oujo said. "The ball got stuck between the catcher's chest protector and his body. OK, the ball is dead immediately, and as I'm screaming the ball is dead, the ball comes through his chest protector and falls out on the ground in front of him. The catcher picked up the ball and threw to third and threw the runner out. But the rule allows the runner one base, so he was awarded third base."

OUJO ALSO REMEMBERS a nightmare situation he encountered during a winter season he spent in the Caribbean.

"I was working in the Dominican Republic and this call delayed the game by a half-hour," Oujo said. "I was working with three of their local umpires.

"The bases were loaded and there was one out. There was a fly ball hit to right field. The first-base umpire went out with the ball. The right fielder appeared to have caught the ball and held it for a second or two, but then lost it. He didn't pull the ball out of the glove.

"The first-base umpire erroneously ruled it a catch. The right fielder gets up thinking that he had dropped the ball, because he didn't see the umpire call the catch. Nobody had seen him call it a catch. The right fielder picks up the ball and throws it to second base trying to force the runner going from first to second there. The second-base umpire, thinking that it was no catch, called the runner out at second on the force. Then World War III erupted.

"What we ended up doing was ruling the fly ball to right the second out and the runner going from second to third out on an appeal play and scored the runner going from third to home.

"That's an example of how an umpire can mess up a play. Manny Mota and Joe Ferguson were the managers and I was umpiring the plate so I ultimately had to make the ruling."

ONE OF THE STRANGEST PLAYS Oujo could recall came not when he was umpiring, but when he was a high school player for Madison Central in Old Bridge, New Jersey.

This play showed once and for all that although players and coaches are always trying to give umpires a helping hand, their help is usually unwelcome.

"We had runners on second and third base and the batter singled to score the runner from third," Oujo recalled. "The runner from third saw that the bat was left near the plate and he tried to go back and retrieve it and get it out of the way, because the runner from second was coming in to score. The umpire should have gotten the bat out of the way, but the runner went back to get it and when the throw came in from the outfield it was up the third-base line a little bit and the catcher ran into the runner who had already scored.

"The umpire had no choice but to call the runner from second out at home for interference."

BRIAN GORMAN

SOUTHERN LEAGUE

Gorman, twenty-seven, is a native of Iselin, New Jersey. He lives in Los Angeles during the off-season. He umpired in the New York–Penn and Florida State leagues before joining the Southern League staff in 1986. Gorman is the son of former major league umpire Tom Gorman.

ONE FUNNY AND UNUSUAL situation arose when Gorman decided to play a practical joke on his Florida State League partner, Charlie Reliford.

The joke didn't start out as one. Reliford explains:

"We pulled into Lakeland real late at night, about two or three in the morning after a long road trip from Miami," Reliford said. "We were so tired I didn't feel like bringing all my stuff in from the car. I just wanted to get to my room and get some sleep.

"The next morning we get up and find that everything has been stolen out of our rental car. Personal clothes, all my umpiring equipment, everything.

"I panicked. I didn't know what to do because I wasn't going to have any stuff to wear. So, I called John Hirschbeck, an American League umpire, and asked him if he had any extra stuff to wear and could he send it to me as quickly as possible.

"Hirschbeck said he did and he would have his wife send it on a cargo plane to me. He lives right outside of Pittsburgh and his wife puts the stuff on the plane and the plane crashes around Pittsburgh.

"So we have to go to the ballpark and my only recourse now is to borrow Brian's gear. Well Brian Gorman is about 6'3" and quite a bit taller than me. So I take his plate uniform and try to make it fit the best I could. I took his pants and turned them up and hemmed them with tape. His shirts were down on my elbows. His hats were too big. His size twelve shoes I had to stuff with cotton to fit my nine and a half feet.

"I looked like Little Orphan Umpire out there. We had the West Palm Beach Expos in that night and they had a catcher by the name of Jim Cecchini who was a pretty fair guy. He didn't give you a lot of static behind the plate and talk too much back there."

That's when Gorman went into action.

"I talked to the catcher and explained what was going on and told him to give Charlie a hard time and I would back him up no matter what he said," Gorman explained.

Reliford picks the narrative up from here.

"When we get out to home plate for the National Anthem, Jim says, 'Gee, Charlie, what's wrong with you, you look terrible,' " Reliford said.

"I tell him, 'Jim, I had all my stuff stolen and I really don't want to talk about it.' He says, 'Don't want to talk about it! This is a professional ballgame out here and look at you! How can you come out here like this?'

"I said, 'Jim, I've really had a bad day and I don't want to talk about it.' He said, 'You better want to talk about it. You're a disgrace. Look at you, how could you come out here like this?'

"I said, 'Jim, look, I told you I had my stuff stolen.' He asked why I didn't go out and buy more. I told him that this stuff was custom-made and you couldn't just walk into a sporting goods store and just buy it off a rack.

Then came the clincher.

Cecchini looked at Reliford with a straight face and said, "Well I'll tell you what. That stuff can't be that hard to find because I've got a friend who lives by the airport in Pittsburgh and he just found a whole big box full of it."

"And stupid me," said Reliford. "I hooked right into it and started yelling right at home plate, 'That's my stuff, that's my stuff.'

Gorman was watching the scene incredulously.

"I looked at Charlie and told him I was about to be mad at Cecchini for not making up a better story—and you still fell for it," Gorman said.

Reliford went most of the remainder of the season without his own plate equipment. He said the experience taught him a lesson.

"Now a lot of the umpires I know keep a spare set of equipment at home in case of something like this happening," Reliford said. "It used to be that I would take any spare piece of equipment I had to spring training with me and give it to an up-and-coming umpire. Now I give away about a third of it and keep the rest of it in case of an emergency."

GORMAN TELLS ANOTHER funny story involving a plane. This incident also occurred during a Florida State League game.

"I was in Fort Lauderdale and I had a close play at first base," Gorman said. "Bucky Dent was their manager and he came out to argue the call at first. There is a private airport right by the field and a plane had taken off and was about five-hundred to six hundred feet in the air and the engine stalled out. You could hear the plane going and then all of sudden you hear it sputtering and it was kind of gliding up there. We're both arguing and then we hear this thing, actually the whole stadium heard it, and everyone looked up. Finally the guy gets the engine started up again and the plane goes off and we went back to arguing.

"I told him, 'Bucky, it could be worse. You could be sitting in that plane up there.'"

SCOTT POTTER

EASTERN LEAGUE

Potter, twenty-five, has been umpiring professionally for six years. A native of Indianapolis, he now makes his home in South Daytona, Florida. He has worked in the Gulf Coast, Appalachian, Florida State and Eastern leagues.

WHILE MUCH OF THE nation laughed in 1987 at the famous "spud caper" pulled off by Dave Bresnahan in the Eastern League, Potter, the home plate umpire during the incident, was not amused in the least.

In case you've forgotten tale number 1 in part 1, Besnahan was a catcher for the Williamsport Bills. He threw a peeled potato into left field on an apparent pickoff attempt to decoy the runner on third into believing he had thrown the ball away.

Bresnahan has had his say. Now let's get the umpire's point of view.

"We were in Williamsport and they were affiliated with the Cleveland Indians," Potter said. "They were playing the Reading Phillies. Basically what happened is that the catcher prefaced it by saying to me before the game that he hoped his mitt would make it through the year. 'I hope it doesn't break,' he said.

"This was the first game of a doubleheader and it was the fifth or sixth inning. We had started forty-five minutes to an hour late because of rain. With one out and Reading's Rick Lundblade running at third, the batter had a count of 1–2. The pitcher throws the ball and strikes the batter out for the second out of the inning. Bresnahan threw the ball back to the pitcher and told me he had broken his glove. Usually a catcher will break his glove four or five times a year, so it's no big deal and I didn't think anything of it.

"Bresnahan went over, got a new glove and came back out. Now

44

there are two outs. The pitcher delivers the ball to the plate. Bresnahan takes what I think at the time is a baseball and throws it into left field in an effort to pick off the runner at third.

"When the runner came toward home Bresnahan came out and tagged him and showed me a baseball. I immediately called the guy safe and I told Bresnahan, 'It doesn't matter. You went to the dugout, you got a baseball, you still can't do that garbage. You can't do it, the run scores.'

"He said, 'But I didn't throw a baseball' and I told him again, 'Dave, you threw a baseball into left field and it doesn't matter, the run scores.'

"About this time his manager comes out and he wants to know what's going on. His manager, Orlando Gomez, is not irate, not arguing my decision or anything like that.

"About this time my partner, John Golden, comes in from third base and he's throwing this object up in the air. It was a potato, but it was basically a little round potato that was shaped like a baseball. The only reason John found out what it was, was because when the ball went into left field and the left fielder went over to pick it up, John said that the guy looked like he was picking up a pile of crap, from the expression on his face.

"John told the left fielder to throw the ball out and when the guy threw it toward the dugout, John noticed that it didn't roll symmetrically or like a baseball should, so John went and picked it up.

"That was basically it. There was no argument from his manager. The manager apologized for him. The guy was fired the next day from the ballclub."

While Bresnahan was given the gate by Williamsport, Potter did not throw him out of the game.

"He probably should have been ejected," Potter said. "But the reason he wasn't ejected was because he was the only catcher they had. He was the only guy who could catch. The only guy they could have put in was a backup second baseman who had never caught before. In hindsight he should have been ejected, but my safety came first. It was not the correct thing to do by any means, but that's what was done."

Potter said he was angry at Bresnahan for using the trick play.

"I was pissed at him. I yelled and screamed at him and initially I thought it was a baseball. I didn't think it was funny at all. What if Rick Lundblade dives back into third base and injures himself and ruins his career? I didn't think it was funny, Reading didn't think it was funny and Orlando Gomez, his manager, didn't think it was funny."

PAM POSTEMA

AMERICAN ASSOCIATION

Postema, thirty-four, is the second woman to become a professional umpire and the only full-time female ump in professional baseball in 1988. She lives in Phoenix, and has twelve years of experience in the Gulf Coast, Florida State, Texas and Pacific Coast leagues, as well as the American Association. She has umpired in Colombia and Puerto Rico during the winter, although she currently spends her off-season working for United Parcel Service.

OVER THE YEARS, baseball's ballboys and ballgirls have saved umpires miles of wear and tear on their legs. These faithful, underappreciated ballpark rats retrieve foul balls to the backstop screen and keep the umpires supplied with fresh baseballs. But, as Postema found out in 1988, these little godsends can also cause confusion.

Postema was calling the plate in a game between the Omaha Royals and Oklahoma City 89ers at Omaha's Rosenblatt Stadium.

The Royals were leading 3–0 in the fifth inning when Oklahoma City pitcher Craig McMurtry threw a high and inside pitch which got by the catcher and went to the screen.

As the Royals' Jose Castro was scoring from third base, a ballboy, thinking the pitch was fouled off, retrieved the ball from the backstop before the 89ers' catcher could get to it.

"The ballboy picked up the ball because he thought it was a foul ball," Postema laughed. "I called time and ruled interference on the ballboy. It really wouldn't have made any difference, but it was the home team batting and I ruled the runner from third out."

Omaha manager Glenn Ezell disputed the call, but it didn't affect the outcome of the game, a 9–0 victory for the Royals.

THOUGH POSTEMA HAS silenced many of her doubters during her twelve years of service in the minor leagues, she has had to endure her share of gender jokes.

"We were in Louisville and the Redbirds' pitching coach, Darold Knowles, had sent a note out with the ballboy that said something like, 'Pam, there's a wet T-shirt contest at such-and-such a bar, how do you think you will do?'" explained Postema's umpiring partner Charlie Reliford.

"Then, later in the game they pulled a great practical joke on her. They took a Dixie cup, the kind they send us water in, and they had taken a hole puncher and punched a hole in the side of the cup. They had the batboy put his thumb over the hole and fill it up with water. So he brings it out and hands it to Pam, who is working the plate, and when he lets go of the hole the water is going all over her. She's turned around waving to the dugout to acknowledge the water and to say thanks for the drink and in the meantime she is getting soaked. It might have been one of those things where you had to be there to really appreciate it, but it was hilarious. The players were laughing. We were laughing. Darold's a pretty fair guy so he was able to get away with it."

EARLY IN THE 1987 American Association schedule, major league substitute umpire Tom Hallion was working with Postema's crew before the big league umpires began taking time off.

"We were in Buffalo and it was cold," said Reliford. "We were all standing at the plate and we were all wearing sweaters, jackets, gloves, everything we could find so you couldn't really tell us apart by our figures.

"Tommy's hair was relatively long for an umpire. He was down in Triple-A getting ready to go to the big leagues. Pam has really short hair. Tom's curly hair was out the back of his hat and some writer came up and tapped him on the shoulder and said, 'Pam, I would like to ask you a few questions.'

"Tommy just said, 'Jeez, now I'm getting mistaken for Pam,' and laughed about it."

RANDY MARSH

NATIONAL LEAGUE

Marsh, thirty-nine, has been umpiring in the National League since 1981 and became a regular in 1982. He was born in Covington, Kentucky and lives in Edgewood, Kentucky. Marsh had the honor of umpiring the 1988 All Star Game in Cincinnati, across the river from his hometown. He is married to the former Roxanne McFarland and has a daughter, Lauren. Marsh attended college at the University of Kentucky and played baseball in high school. He previously umpired in the Appalachian, Florida State, Eastern and Pacific Coast leagues, as well as in the Florida Instructional League and the Dominican Republic winter league. During the off-season, Marsh is a national representative for a sporting goods company and enjoys photography and golf as hobbies.

MARSH FOUND OUT in the Pacific Coast League that a manager's actions can sometimes speak louder than his words. Let him explain:

"When I was in the Pacific Coast League I had a play that involved Rene Lachemann, who went on to manage in the big leagues," Marsh said. "Rene worked at Dodger Stadium as a kid. In fact he took care of the umpires' room at one time. So he got to know all the umpires and he was always a real fair guy.

"He was managing Spokane before he got his big league job and their team was just playing really bad. Their fans were all over them. I was on the bases and I was working with Larry Poncino.

"Spokane had Jerry Narron on first base, and he ran like he had a piano on his back. Narron was going on the pitch and the batter hit the pitch behind him to right field. All Narron knew was the ball was behind him.

"The second baseman was running over toward us and the short-stop was yelling, 'Give it to me, give it to me,' acting like he was going for the double play.

"Narron slid, but the ball was in right field. He got up and realized what was going on and ran to third base but he had not come near second yet. When he stood up he was probably ten feet from second base. When he got up and ran he was running along the edge of the infield grass. He was not anywhere in the vicinity of second base.

"So they appealed second base and I called him out. Lachemann was the manager and at that time a lot of Triple-A managers coached third base. There may be a thousand people in the stands and he comes out throws his hands in the air and says: 'You know what, you and Poncino have been busting your ass this whole series and you've been doing a hell of a job.'

"The people in the stands are thinking he's giving me all kinds of crap. He goes on and goes on and says, 'If my guys were busting their ass as much as you guys are and were paying attention as much as you guys are, we'd be playing a lot better baseball.'

"So everybody really thinks he's getting me good now. I'm covering my mouth, trying not to laugh at the guy. Finally he says, 'Now when you want me to get the hell out of here, you just tell me because I'll get the hell off the field.'

"He starts to get real animated now and he begins to point his finger and he begins to take his hat off and I said, 'Don't throw your hat because I'll have to dump you, and besides, these fans are really starting to get on my tail now. I really think it's time for you to get out of here.' "

"He said all right, and he takes a few steps away from me and turns around and he points at me and he says, 'You're doing a hell of a job,' And he went back over to the third-base coaching box and pointed at the batter to go ahead and hit. Then I looked over at him and he tipped his hat to me as if to say thanks.

"At the end of the inning he's running across the infield and I'm going across the infield, he gets my attention and puts his hands up in the air maybe three feet apart and said, 'He missed second base by this much.' And the fans still think he's just continuing to get on my ass.

"If it had been anybody but him and knowing how he was with umpires, I probably wouldn't have put up with that much. But he was always such a fair guy he really didn't give us a hard time at all, he would just let you umpire and do your job."

THE HOTFOOT IS one of the oldest practical jokes in baseball, but Marsh remembered having another foot joke played on him when he was a beginning umpire.

"There was a guy who played in the Giants' organization named Skip James," Marsh recalled. "He was a great first baseman, but he was stuck behind Willie McCovey. The year the Giants were going to take him up was the year McCovey decided he was going to go back and play for the Giants, so they ended up trading Skip to Milwaukee, and *they* had Cecil Cooper playing first for them.

"[Skip] was an outstanding first baseman. I think he held a lot of records for the Phoenix Giants at Triple-A. And he was a real decent guy who hardly ever gave umpires any static.

"One thing about Skip was that his shoes were always immaculate. They were always shined perfectly. The orange stripes were always clean. He was Mr. Prim-and-Proper as far as his shoes were concerned.

"At that time I was getting close to the big leagues. And some of the big league umpires when they signed new shoe contracts would give me a pair of their new shoes.

"So Skip sees me wearing this pair of new Adidas umpiring shoes. They were high-top umpiring shoes with a blue stripe on the side of them.

"Skip said, 'Real nice shoes. Are those house slippers or are those plate shoes?' He was just busting my chops and I didn't think anything of it.

"That was when we were in Phoenix and then we went to Albuquerque and the Giants are playing there. I'm working the game and Skip comes up and again says, 'Real nice shoes.'

"He keeps making these little comments about them the whole

game and I can't figure out why he's dwelling on it. I work the game and then walk off the field and find out when I get to the locker room that on the bottom of my shoes is a piece of white athletic tape on each shoe running from the heel all the way to the toe. On each piece of tape was written, 'Nice shoes.'

"Now when I ran during the game I had to look like a damn zebra out there with these white stripes on the bottom of my shoes. Everybody was laughing like hell the whole game and I was the only one that didn't know about it."

VIC TRAVIS

INTERNATIONAL LEAGUE, RETIRED

Travis, thirty-seven, worked in the minor leagues for six years, umpiring in the Appalachian, Carolina, Southern and International leagues. Although he retired from professional umpiring, he still works amateur games around his hometown of Lexington, Kentucky. Travis is married with three children, and now works as a deputy sheriff in Lexington, runs a winter umpiring school and helps run a trophy company.

TRAVIS HAD DOUBLE TROUBLE during a game he umpired in the Southern League when two players wound up on third base. He said he is still not sure if he and his partner Larry Vanover made the right call on the play.

"To this day I don't know if we got it right or not," Travis prefaced his story. "We were calling a game in Double-A between the Charlotte Orioles, with manager John Hart, and the Knoxville Blue Jays, with their manager, John McLaren. I was working the bases and Larry had the plate. We had a hit to the outfield and a Blue Jay named Kash Beauchamp slid into third base. A guy was coming back to third so we had double runners on third base. I called Beauchamp out, pointed at him and told him he was out.

"Well, McLaren had started yelling at Beauchamp for running the other guy off the base. Then the other guy on third begins to walk off the base and in Knoxville, their dugout set real close up to the plate and this guy just starts walking down the third base chalk line.

"Well, the pitcher goes over and almost starts to tag him, but doesn't. It's like he thought the wrong guy was walking off the base, but Beauchamp was still standing at third because McLaren was chewing him out. I'm getting ready to call a double play if the pitcher tags him, but he never did.

"The runner just keeps walking right down the line and he keeps kind of looking back and I'm thinking, is he abandoning the base or is he just trying to deke [decoy] everybody? He continues to walk right down the line and he gets to the plate—and he steps right over it without touching it.

"Well, now they say something to Larry and I don't know what they're saying but he puts his arms up like in a safe sign so I'm thinking, 'We've got a run scored.' That becomes Larry's call now of whether he touched the plate.

"Well I'm looking at Larry and I'm thinking, he knows what I've got, and I think we're communicating and that Larry has called him safe and we've got the run scored.

"The runner walks into the dugout and sits down and everything and John Hart runs out and says, 'Vic, that's the wrong guy on third base.'

"I looked at Larry and asked him if he had a safe call at the plate and he said no and I asked him if he had called time out and he said no. Then I looked in the dugout and told the runner he was out for abandoning the base.

"Well there was some question about that because the rules say if they go fifteen to twenty feet away from the base or if it's a considerable difference that the runner can be called out for abandoning the base. But, since he walked right down the basepath, he gave us no indication he was abandoning the base. If he had been dekeing everybody and stepped on the plate they would have scored a run. By walking off the base and making no attempt to step on the plate you could call him out for abandoning.

"I've asked several different people and some of my friends who are umpires in the big leagues and they've said, 'Oh boy.' It was a catch-22 situation. We were damned if we do and damned if we don't.

"That call has always stuck out in my mind because I've always wondered whether I got the call wrong or got it right."

TRAVIS REMEMBERS ANOTHER strange situation he and his partner were involved in, but they were luckily spared a possible protest.

"I was working in the Appalachian League and the season was almost over," said Travis, who did not wish to reveal the identity of his partner because of possible embarrassment. "We had a game between Johnson City and Bristol and they were down in the cellar of the league. My partner and I had a great season and this was the day before the season was going to be over. There was a runner at first base and the batter hit an apparent double to the outfield.

"The [Johnson City] Cardinals made a play on the guy going to second and it was a whacker [a close play] and my partner called him safe. When he did call him safe their second baseman started screaming and hollering. In the meantime the guy who was on first has rounded third and is coming hard toward home.

"Well now the second baseman reacts and throws to home. The throw is way off the mark and the run scores. But, after the call at second and the argument began, my partner had called time out before the play was actually dead.

"As soon as the runner slid at home I told him he would have to go back to third. The runner said, 'What do you mean,' and I told him that time was called at second and once the ball was dead he couldn't advance.

"Well the Bristol manager [Boots Day] comes out and is arguing that the run should count and my partner comes in and tells me that it was his mistake and he was going to allow the run. I told him he couldn't do that, but he insisted that he wasn't going to let his mistake cost the team a run. I told him if he did that we could expect a protest.

"He said he didn't give a damn, that if they did protest he would keep me clear of it and would report in any paperwork to the league office that I had tried to talk him out of it.

"Well, I couldn't talk him out of it and he allowed the run to score. This is in the second inning and, sure enough, Rich Hacker [the Cardinals manager] comes out and tells me that he had all his bosses there and they had just chewed his butt out that morning for not winning with players like Vince Coleman and Terry Pendleton, so he was going to have to protest the game.

"So I tried to talk to my partner again and he said he was going to allow the run to score and that was it. So I said OK, Hacker protested the game and I signaled to the scorekeeper that the game was being played under protest.

"That happened in the second inning and you could hear thunder and lightning off in the distance and finally it begins to rain in the third inning. When we get into the dressing room my partner realizes that he has screwed up and told me he should have listened to me.

"It stops raining, which irritates us more because we thought we might get rained out and this protest is not going to go through, and we have to go back onto the field.

"In the fourth inning another rain comes and we've got to pull them off the field again. It stops again and we go out to check the field again. Well the manager of the [Bristol] Tigers comes over to us and said, "You guys have done a hell of a job all year and I would hate to see you end your season with a protest. But, I'll tell you what, right now we've had two rain delays and if you bang [call off] this son-of-a-gun right now we can get to the beer before the bars shut down.'

"And that manager was ahead, but his team was in last place. Hacker came out and said 'You think it's too wet to play?' and I said yes and he said 'Me too,' and he looked at me with this big smile on his face.

"I said, 'Screw it, that's it.' Boom, I banged it and we walked out of there so the protest never did take effect. We got out of that one with a break."

While Travis got a good break to end the Appalachian League season that year, he didn't get any slack when he began his Triple-A umpiring career in the International League.

"I was working with Tony Maners and Terry Craft my first year of Triple-A and I had just got moved up," Travis explained. "Tony was a big practical joker and I was in getting dressed when the guy came in to get the umpiring lineup for the press box. Tony told the guy, 'It'll be me, Tony Maners, working behind the plate, Terry Craft will be on third and we've got a new guy named Al Cohol doing first.

"Well the guy doesn't catch the joke and he walks on out. So they announce the lineup and who's working and over the public address system they said Al Cohol would be working first base. Well the fans went nuts. The game was in Syracuse and I've got a videotape of the game and the local television announcers went for four innings calling me Al Cohol on the broadcast.

"When the announcers come back the next night to do a television game they realized it was a practical joke and they told the story on the air the next night."

RICK DARBY

SOUTHERN LEAGUE, RETIRED

Darby and his wife, Kim, live in Inverness, Florida, where Rick is now umpiring college and other amateur games when he's not coaching or teaching at Hernando High School. Darby worked in the Appalachian, Florida State and Southern leagues as an umpire before he retired after 1987. He is thirty-three years old.

Darby said one of the strangest situations he ever encountered was a Southern League play in which he got more than he bargained for. This was one play that was gone with the wind.

"Vic Travis, Larry Vanover and I were working a game in Double-

A between the Twins team [Orlando] and the Oakland team [Huntsville]," Darby explained. "I was working first base, Vic had third and Larry had the plate.

"There was a little pop-up behind second base that was a 'tweener in front of the outfield but beyond the infielders. When the ball was hit I looked at Vic and he was going out with the ball to see if it was caught. The shortstop went out on the play and he was a former major leaguer. The left fielder and the center fielder were also coming in on the ball and the second baseman was going out on it, also. Well, you couldn't have placed the ball any more perfectly.

"Well [Huntsville's] Stan Javier was the batter and he runs like a deer. When I see Vic go out I come in and pivot to get a good angle on first base and I'm figuring that from where the ball is going to fall that there's a good chance that Javier is going to go to second base and I'm going to have to make that call.

"I think the center fielder ended up with the ball, but there was nobody covering second base so Javier goes to second. By now the third baseman had seen what was going on so he went over to cover second. Since there was nobody there the outfielder had to lead him with the throw so he really couldn't put anything on it.

"Well, Javier looks up and he's already at second base and he is not even thinking about slowing down, and the ball is just now getting there. He looks over to third and there is nobody there either. The third baseman tried to tag him but by the time he tried to swipe the tag on him, Javier was already five or six feet past him.

"I've never seen anything like it. Javier goes to third base and now the catcher tries to get there to cover the base. Well, the same thing happens. The throw gets to the catcher about the same time Javier is hitting the base and now nobody is covering home and he blows by the catcher just like he did the third baseman at second and goes on to score. He had turned a single into an inside-the-park home run and here I was just following him around the bases."

EEENIE, MEENIE, MINEY, MO. Which Mike has got to go?

Darby found himself in a perplexing situation when he was umpiring a game in the Appalachian League during his rookie year.

"We were in Paintsville, Kentucky, where the Yankees had a farm club," Darby explained. "There was a close play at first base and I might have missed it. Well, the Yankees' dugout was just a few feet away from first base and they're letting me have it.

"When I looked up in their dugout I noticed a couple of guys in there that weren't in uniform. They were the grounds crew and they're all over me. Well, I told them they had to get out of there, and while they're leaving the Yankees coaches are still all over my ass."

The Paintsville manager, Mike Easom, and coaches Mike Notaro and Mike McLeod were all sitting together in folding chairs just outside the dugout.

"Finally I had enough and I said, 'Mike, you're done.' "

None of the Paintsville coaches budged. Instead, they calmly sat there and asked Darby, "Which one?"

"Hell I didn't really know one from the other," Darby admitted. "It was a rookie league with a seventy-game schedule and there wasn't much publicity in those leagues so you really didn't get to know the players and managers like you do in most leagues. I knew the manager's name was Easom so I said Mike Easom had to go.

"He comes out and gets in my face and asked me why I was throwing him out of the game. I told him I hadn't yet, and he informed me that he was Mike Easom.

"Well most rookie league managers also coach third base, but he didn't. The other guy, Notaro, coached third and also brought out the lineup and I just assumed he was the manager. When Easom came out and told me he was the manager I just told him I meant the other son-of-a-gun sitting over there and that he was gone."

So Darby had given Notaro and the grounds crew the gate, but the story didn't end there.

"My partner was Vic Travis and when I ran the grounds crew one of them told me he was going to get me," Darby explained. "Vic was an instigator and when we got to the dressing room after the game he started trying to scare me.

"He said, 'You know, big man, these mountain people mean it when they make a threat like that. You might want to watch yourself. I'll tell you what, when I go take my shower I'll lock the door behind me and don't open it for anybody else but me. These guys are crazy, they might try to kill you.'

"Well the groundskeepers were a couple of brothers, and they weren't really very threatening. But the more he kept talking about it and the more I thought about it the madder I got, and I told him nobody was going to keep me from taking a shower when I wanted to. About that time one of the brothers went by the dressing room and said good-bye and that was the end of it."

AL SOMERS

PACIFIC COAST LEAGUE, RETIRED

Somers, eighty-three, umpired in the minor leagues for twenty-two years and was deeply involved in umpiring for thirty-seven years. He took over Bill McGowan's School for Umpires and operated it from 1953 until he passed it on to Harry Wendelstedt in 1977. Somers also was commissioned by the armed services to conduct umpiring clinics overseas during the early '60s.

He was born in Shenandoah, Pennsylvania, and worked in the North Carolina State League, Inter-State League, Eastern League, Southern Association, American Association and the Pacific Coast League, where he was the league's umpire-in-chief.

Somers was inducted as a member of the Pennsylvania Sports Hall of Fame in 1980. He trained more than sixty-five hundred umpires, including more than sixty who reached the major leagues.

"He has revolutionized the training of umpires," Wendelstedt said. "Before him, umpiring schools basically consisted of sitting in classrooms and reading the rulebook."

SOMERS SAID THE strangest play he ever called was a screwy, inning-ending double play on which a run scored.

"I was the plate umpire when it happened to me in Los Angeles, which was in the Cubs' organization in the PCL," Somers said. "The bases were loaded and a fly ball was hit to right field against Joe Gordon's team [San Francisco]. Los Angeles had three men on base and the ball hit to right looked like a base hit to short right field. The right fielder came in and made a great catch. The runner from third had come in to score. He thought it was a hit and he was standing there at the plate saying, 'Oooh, they will probably make the other out.' "

And the (San Francisco) outfielder did throw the ball into second base to catch the runner from second before he could retreat to the bag.

"The runner from third had already crossed the plate, and after they made the third out at second base I turned to the scorer and stuck one finger up and told him to count the run.

"Gordon came barging out onto the field and said, 'No way.' They called down from the press box, trying to figure out what had happened. I told them that they hadn't appealed the play at third base about the runner leaving early, to get the 'fourth out' to supersede the third out, which was made at second."

Since there was no force play at second base, and the runner from third scored before the third out was recorded, the run counts [Rule 4.09]. However, if San Francisco had appealed the fact that the runner on third left too soon, the 'fourth out' on the appeal would have replaced the out at second base, and the run would not have counted [Rule 7.10]. The key is, an appeal must be made.

"They couldn't believe it," Somers said. "So my dressing room was loaded after the game with newsmen. When Gordon came up to the plate and started arguing with me I told him I didn't want to throw him out of the game, but that if he wanted to protest he should.

"Gordon protested the game and he called Joe Cronin (then the president of the Baseball Rules Committee) about the play. Gordon explained the play to him and told him what happened and Cronin asked him, 'Who was the umpire?' Gordon told him, 'It was Al Somers,' and Cronin said, 'You lose. He has all of the rules of baseball down pat. He's been running the umpiring school.'

"Gordon came up to the plate the next night and told me he would never question another call by me."

THAT CALL WAS ONE of many unpopular decisions Somers made in his career. Somers looked like a villain for a day in 1952 as he became part of the Picture of the Week in *Life* magazine.

"I was umpiring the plate on a Mother's Day game and we had a tie game in the ninth inning," Somers said. "During the last inning a woman came out of the stands, walked onto the field and was offering me her glasses. I guess she didn't agree with my calls."

Somers wanted to get on with the ballgame so he looked for a security guard to escort the lady from the field. He motioned with his thumb for a guard to get the lady out of there, and an opportunistic photographer snapped a picture of what appeared to be Somers ejecting the woman from the game.

"I didn't throw her out of there," Somers said. "I was just telling the guard to take her off the field. It was a nothing-nothing game through nine innings."

The following year the Los Angeles club sent another woman out to the plate when Somers was working on Mother's Day in an attempt to draw more national publicity. But Somers was ready for her this time.

"They sent a lady out and she brought me an apple this time and I gave her a watch," Somers laughed. "They tried to get back in a national magazine again, but it didn't work."

BALLPARK ORGANISTS and public address announcers keep the fans entertained between innings and during other slow moments. But umpires don't always think the sideshows are amusing or entertaining. It seems like every year, someone gets in trouble by playing "Three Blind Mice" or some other crowd favorites after a close call by an umpire.

In 1988, for example, a public address announcer in El Paso was ejected from the premises for playing the Linda Ronstadt tune, "When Will I be Loved" after a controversial play. The song just happens to include the refrain, "I've been cheated, been mistreated." And in Omaha, umpire Tony Maners ejected organist Lambert Bartak for playing the Mickey Mouse Club theme song during a rhubarb. "He was playing music derogatory to the profession of umpiring," Maners said.

This kind of thing has been going on for a long, long time. Somers remembers one incident:

"It was in San Diego," Somers said of the infamous "Three Blind Mice" jingle in 1957. "I heard them playing it and I stopped the game and told them to stop playing it or we were going to leave the field. And they cut it out. They've stopped that in the major leagues, too."

SOMERS ALSO REMEMBERS one instance in which fans actually offered him and his partner, "Steamboat" Johnson, something useful.

"We were in Birmingham and Steamboat, who had written a book about umpiring, gets there early for the ballgame," Somers said. "I was supposed to work the plate that night and when I get to the ballpark Johnson is there selling his book and he's selling it for a dollar apiece.

"So we go to the locker room and get dressed and go out and work the game and he has the bases and I'm behind the plate. So, on the first call he has at first base the guy is out and he calls him safe against the home team. So, you guessed it, they're throwing all these books out on the field at us. Well they're throwing them at me, too, so I walk out to second base and [Steamboat] yells over to the groundskeepers to gather the books and to put them in our dressing room.

"After the game I get into the locker room and ask him what is the matter with him. I asked him what he was going to do with all those books and he said, 'Al, we're going to Memphis and I'm going to sell them there and I'm going to pull the same trick.' "

WITH MANY YEARS OF umpiring come many years of travel. The miles were certainly not all carefree. Somers said one rough road trip quickly came to mind.

While the veteran umpire made the most of his modest upbringing—he completed only a fifth-grade education and worked in the coal mines of Pennsylvania—nobody exactly mistook him for a rocket scientist.

Almost nobody, that is.

Somers and his partner were selected to umpire the PCL all-star game in 1954. They had called a game in Los Angeles the night prior to the all-star game.

"I called a limousine to pick us up at the hotel to take us to the airport to go to the all-star game," Somers said. "We asked the guy who came and picked us up to get our bags, and he saw those big suitcases. So he loaded them up and he thought we had instruments to make the atomic bomb. We're going out to the airport and I thought he must be taking a shortcut or something so I didn't say anything for a while. Then we keep going and I finally tell him, 'I think you're making a mistake here.'

"He said, 'Oh no, I know where I'm going.' Well we drive there and he had to have a pass to get in there. It was an atomic project. Finally he goes in and comes back out and said we were in the wrong place and I told him that was what I had said in the first place.

"We were supposed to be on our way to San Diego and we get to the airport late and had to call the airplane back. The people at the airport called the plane back, it was getting ready to take off and when we got on the plane, the players were razzing us pretty good."

DUTCH RENNERT

NATIONAL LEAGUE

Dutch is his nickname, but his real name is Laurence Henry Rennert, Jr., and he hails from Vero Beach, Florida—the spring training home of the Los Angeles Dodgers. Rennert, fifty-four, is married to the former Shirley Malchow and has four children, Jeff, Greg, Kevin and Melissa. Rennert was a three-sport athlete in high school, playing football, basketball and baseball. He began his major league umpiring career in 1973 and became a regular staff member in 1974. He previously umpired in the Alabama-Florida, Pioneer, Three-I, Texas and Pacific Coast leagues, as well as the Southern Association.

RENNERT SAID he has some fond memories of the years he spent in the minors. A case of mistaken identity led to one of Rennert's most embarrassing moments as an umpire.

"I was working in the Pioneer League in the low minors," Rennert said. "It was a class C league when they used to have them organized A, B, C and D.

"There was a player named Frank Franchi, and when you didn't play in the minor leagues then you took turns coaching the bases. This guy Franchi was a catcher, and he was one of those guys that was hard to get along with. In the old days everybody was hard to get along with. I had always kind of waited for the opportunity, but I never got a shot to eject him and pick him off.

"Franchi played for Idaho Falls and their manager was a guy named Al Lakeman, a real good guy who used to pitch for the Detroit Tigers. One night everybody is yelling and screaming like they usually do in the minors and I looked in their dugout. It's tough to see in the dugouts in the minors because the lighting is usually not too good and I finally said, 'OK, Franchi, you're through, get out of the dugout, you're done playing for tonight.'

"Well, Lakeman comes up to the plate real slow and calm and says, 'Dutch, I've got news for you. Franchi is coaching first base.' And I turned around and there he was coaching first base. So here's the topper, I said, 'I'm sorry Al, I thought it was Franchi, it was the second guy from the right,' and it turned out to be a guy named Charlie Strange, a third baseman, super guy who never said 'boo' to anyone, and he gets ejected.

"That was embarrassing, but I learned something that day. Don't just go by voices."

RENNERT ALSO REMEMBERS one holiday game that got him as hot as a firecracker.

"This game was back in the Pioneer League as well," Rennert said. "We traveled in pairs in that league and the ballparks are very small and old. One time, at a July 4 game, the grounds crew guy thought we were out on the diamond and locked us in the tunnel underneath home plate.

"We couldn't get out and nobody even thought to come and get us out. Nobody could figure it out where we were, they must have thought we were out getting a beer or something. We ended up being about twenty minutes late and the ballgame got started twenty minutes late because of it. All I could think about afterward was if there had been a fire we would have been done for down there.

"In the big leagues things like that don't happen because you have so much security and things, but the minor leagues were fun and there are a lot of great stories."

OF COURSE, RENNERT ALSO had his obligatory minor league travel nightmare.

"We had a few accidents in cars with all the driving we did in the minor leagues," Rennert said. "I remember one time in Oklahoma on the open range we hit a cow. Luckily, the ballclub was behind us on the bus and picked us up and took us to Tulsa for the ballgame."

The ballplayers, naturally, couldn't let the opportunity pass to get a few digs in at Rennert and his umpiring partner.

"Oh yeah, they said, 'You can't see nothing as it is, how are you going to see a cow in the middle of the road?' But I'll tell you, on the open range there at night it is tough to see and they just wander right across the road. My partner was a guy named Bob Henry, and it really messed up his car."

JERRY LAYNE

PACIFIC COAST LEAGUE

Layne is thirty years old and has been umpiring for eleven years. He began his arbiting career in the Appalachian League and has worked in the Florida State, Southern and Pacific Coast leagues. Layne is an instructor at the Harry Wendelstedt School for Umpires. He and his wife, Jackie, live in Winter Haven, Florida, with their two-year-old daughter, Brittany.

LAYNE, LIKE ALL OTHER umpires, often has his eyesight questioned by some of baseball's less sophisticated fans.

The managers and players get in their digs as well. Ironically, one manager nearly made Layne legally blind during a serious incident in 1986.

"The weirdest thing that ever happened to me as an umpire was when I had Pam Postema as a partner and we got in an argument with Larry Bowa," Layne said.

"I was in the Pacific Coast League. Pam was working the plate and she had reversed her call on a hit batter. First she called foul ball, but when the batter showed her the mark the ball left on his arm or hand, she awarded the batter first base.

"The call went against Bowa's team and the game was in Las Vegas and it was his home field. He had already been ejected by her once or twice that season prior to this.

"I was working on what *USA Today* termed as the Mod Squad,

62

after a television series about ten years ago. Our other partner was Chuck Meriwether, a black umpire.

"Well we get in a real rhubarb with Bowa and he's going at Pam pretty good. By that time she had already ejected him for arguing too long and he was really mad. She had just ejected him a few series before and he was really trying to watch his p's and q's. But he really didn't know what he could get away and not get away with because it was his first year of managing.

"Well he thought he had been run for no reason and things were starting to get violent so Chuck and I went down the line to separate Bowa and Pam. He was going berserk and we physically had to restrain him from her. As we did so we were still in the home plate area and he proceeded to start kicking dirt.

"Well, when he started doing that we just started backing off the dirt area, to where he couldn't kick any dirt. As we were backing up he kicked the loose dirt in the batter's box where they dig in and when he did he sprayed all three of us umpires with the dirt and we looked like a bunch of Dalmatian dogs with spots all over us.

"This piece of dirt that had chalk or lime or whatever was used to line the batter's box got in my eye. I went over to the trainer and he tried to get it out, but he couldn't. He could see it up in my eye, but couldn't get to it.

"They sent me to the emergency room and to make a long story short I ended up missing almost thirty days of work, because less than a week after that I was still legally blind in my left eye. I couldn't even read the front page of the newspaper."

GERRY DAVIS

NATIONAL LEAGUE

The thirty-five-year-old Davis was born in St. Louis, Missouri, and now resides in Appleton, Wisconsin. He has been umpiring in the National League since 1983 and became a regular member of the staff in 1985. He has also umpired in the Midwest League, Eastern League, American Association, Florida Instructional League and the Puerto Rican winter league. During the off-season Davis does some public relations work for the Wisconsin Flyers of the Continental Basketball Association. He also plays golf, skis and officiates basketball games. He is married to the former Lynn Mentzel.

THE MOST UNUSUAL CALL that Davis can remember in his career involved the other woman. The other woman umpire, that is.

"I was in the minor leagues and my partner was Christine Wren, the only professional woman umpire at the time," Davis explained.

"We were working in the Midwest League and we were in Clinton, Iowa, and they were playing the Quad City club from Davenport, Iowa.

"Quad City had the bases loaded with nobody out and they hit a ball to straightaway center field that the runners felt had not been caught. In fact, it had been.

"The runners were running on the pitch and all of a sudden the third base coach realized the ball had been caught and the center fielder was throwing the ball back in. The runner from first had reached third by then and he thought the quickest way back to first was straight across the field. He went back across the mound. He didn't bother going back to second.

"Well the throw came into third where they appealed that the runner had left too early for the second out, and the runner who crossed over the mound was called out for making a travesty of the game.

"The Quad City manager was Chuck Cottier and he was coaching third base. He went nuts. That was an unusual triple play and it took us about fifteen or twenty minutes to explain what had happened to whom."

PART THREE
HYPOTHETICAL HORRORS

NINETY QUESTIONS THAT WILL
TEST YOUR KNOWLEDGE
OF THE RULES

It is often said life is stranger than fiction. That is not always the case.

On the following pages you will find some ninety hypothetical situations conjured by our panel of experts.

Have these situations ever occurred? Maybe.

Will they? It's possible.

Could they? Sure.

You see something different every time you go to the ballpark. That's one of the things that makes baseball such a great game.

Of course, many of these are things you would rather not see if you're the umpire.

Since these are dreamed-up situations we have used fictional characters from baseball's literature and cinema to represent many of the participants. Our stable of talent includes everybody from Roy Hobbs of *The Natural* to Stud Cantrell and the Tampico Stogies of the movie *Long Gone*. We've filled out the balance of the questions with some of the greatest names and nicknames of all time, selected from the bible of baseball, *The Baseball Encyclopedia*.

KEEPING SCORE ON YOURSELF—FROM THE BUSHES TO THE BIGS!

Be sure to pay attention to your inning-by-inning tally, because at the end of this section you'll be able to grade yourself on just how well you make the call. Tally up your individual score for each of the nine innings and add those scores up when you're through. Give yourself one point for each correct answer; don't subtract any points for incorrect rulings.

Just like Don Denkinger or Pam Postema, you can attempt to advance to the big leagues.

The great thing is, no one will spit tobacco juice on your shoes.

And you may learn something—we'll cite or paraphrase the actual rules to back up the answers.

So, if you're ready, make certain you have all your gear on, rub up a few game balls, and . . .

Let's play ball!

FIRST INNING

1. Jamie Don Weeks triples with one out in the bottom of the ninth inning of a tie game. Stud Cantrell follows him in the Tampico Stogies' lineup. The Dothan Cardinals bring their infield in to cut off the run at the plate. Cantrell rips a line drive down the third-base line past a diving third baseman, but Weeks gets hit with the ball while standing in fair territory and the ball bounds through the hole between shortstop and third. Weeks limps home with the apparent winning run. Safe or out? It's your call.

2. Bump Bailey singles with no outs and is followed in the lineup by Roy Hobbs. Hobbs smacks a hard one-hopper at the opponents' first baseman. Bailey retreats to the bag, thinking it will be caught on the line drive. Realizing he has no chance of reaching second now since the first baseman has the ball, Bailey decides to stay on first base. The first baseman steps on first base and then tags Bailey. Is Bailey out for not trying to advance a base or do the Knights have one out and Bailey still on first? It's your call.

3. Tony Mullane, known to his legion of fans as "The Apollo of the Box," is on third base with Gentleman George Hallock on second for the Forest City nine. Mullane gets a big lead and attempts to steal home. Hallock is napping at second base and does not attempt to steal third. As Mullane crosses the plate on the stolen base attempt, he is hit with the pitch in the strike zone. Is the pitch a ball or strike? Is the runner out for being hit with the pitch? What do you do with the runner on second base? It's your call.

4. Skipper Grammock sends Buford Ellenbogen in to pinch-hit. As you, the umpire, are writing down Ellenbogen's name, but haven't notified the scorer, Grammock changes his mind and decides to pinch-hit Narvel Adams instead. Can Grammock make this change now and can he use Ellenbogen to pinch-hit later if he wishes? What if you had already motioned to the scorer, but no announcement had been made? What if you had motioned and an announcement had been made? It's your call.

5. "Old Aches and Pains," Luke Appling, rips a curling line drive down the right field line in fair territory. The right fielder attempts a diving catch, but wet grounds cause him to slide too far and the ball bounces off the bottom of his spikes and into the short right field bleachers. Home run or ground-rule double? It's your call.

6. Sam "Babe Ruth's Legs" Byrd steps up to the plate and takes a mighty cut at an "Available" Jones fastball. Catcher Red McKee accidentally sticks his catcher's mitt in the way and tips the bat. Byrd still manages to get his swing through quickly enough to knock the ball over the fence. Should Byrd be awarded only first base because of the interference or should the homer stand? It's your call.

7. Xavier "Mr. X" Rescigno is pitching for Chicago when a game is suspended because of darkness. Before the game can be completed Rescigno is traded to another National League team. Coincidentally, Rescigno is traded to the team Chicago had played during the suspended game and is scheduled to start when the game is resumed. Can his new team use him to pitch in a game he was already in for the opposing team? It's your call.

8. Deacon Scott is on first base with the score tied 4–4 in the ninth inning with two outs. Scott breaks for second on a hit-and-run play and "Dynamo" Chiozza executes perfectly by hitting the ball to the hole left by the vacating second baseman. But Scott's helmet flies off as he races for second base and the ball caroms off the headgear and kicks down the right field line, allowing Scott to come all the way around from first to score the apparent winning run. Do you allow the run or call Jackson out for interference? It's your call.

9. Dim Dom Dallessandro makes a diving play on a ball hit up the middle with a runner on first. Dallessandro does not handle the ball cleanly and lunges for second base with his glove hand after picking the ball up with his bare hand and beats the runner. Is the runner out or is he safe because Dallessandro didn't have the ball in his glove when he tagged the bag? It's your call.

10. Pitcher Hal "Ace" Elliott starts thinking about dinner while on the mound and he forgets there is a runner on second base. Suddenly he begins to pitch from a windup. The runner, who had already decided to steal, gets a huge jump toward third and actually reaches third base before Elliott releases the ball. The batter pops up the ball to the infield and it is caught. The second baseman then throws the ball to the shortstop who steps on second base to force the runner who did not tag. The runner, who thought he already had third base stolen, attempts

only to return there. Is the runner out or should he be allowed to remain on third base? It's your call.

Check the first-inning answers on the following pages. See how many you called correctly and write your score for this inning in the first inning box in the scoreboard in the back of the book before the umpire promotion schedule. Now you can continue with your umpire training.

FIRST INNING ANSWERS

1. Because the infielder was in front of the runner, Jamie Don is not out. (Rule 7.08f—Any runner is out when he is touched by a fair ball in fair territory *before* the ball has touched or passed an infielder, and no other infielder has a play on the ball.)

2. One out, Bailey remains on first. The force was removed as soon as the batter-runner was retired. The runner originally on first was legally forced to run but did not physically have to do so (Rule 7.08e). A variation of this question would occur if the first baseman were to tag the runner originally on first, who was now standing on the bag, before the first baseman stepped on first. Then it would become a double play. The original runner lost his legal right to first base because of the force of the batter becoming a runner.

3. The runner stealing is safe since he touched the plate. The fact that he was hit with the pitch does not put him out. The plate umpire should call the pitch a strike in this case as it was in the strike zone. The umpire also should allow the runner on second base to go to third base even though he was merely standing there and made no attempt to steal. (Rule 5.09h—If any legal pitch touches a runner trying to score, runners advance.)

4. According to recent interpretation of rule 3.06, the substitute is in the game as soon as the manager announces the change to the umpire. If Grammock were to change his mind, Ellenbogen would still be done for the day. It doesn't make any difference whether or not the umpire has notified the official scorer.

5. Home run. The ball is still in flight off of a defensive player. (Rule 2.00—*In flight* describes a batted or thrown or pitched ball that has not yet touched the ground or some object other than a fielder.)

6. Home run. (Rule 6.08c—The batter becomes a runner and is entitled to first base when the catcher or any other fielder interferes

with him. If a play follows the interference the manager of the offense may address the plate umpire that he elects to decline the interference penalty and accept the play. Such election shall be made immediately after the play. However, if the batter reaches first base on a hit, error, a base on balls, a hit batsman or otherwise *and* all runners advance a base the play proceeds without reference to the interference.)

7. Yes, the pitcher can play for the opposing team. (Rule 4.12*d*— Any player who was not with the club when the game was suspended may be used as a substitute even if he has taken the place of a player no longer with the club who would not have been eligible because he had been removed from the lineup before the game was suspended.)

8. Allow the run. If a batted ball strikes a helmet *accidentally*, with no intent on the part of the runner, the ball remains in play as if it had not hit the helmet.

9. This is a force play, the runner is out. (Rule 2.00—A *tag* is the action of a fielder in touching the base with any part of his body while holding the ball securely and firmly in his hand or glove; or touching a runner with the ball, or with his hand or glove holding the ball securely and firmly in his hand or glove.)

10. Out. The position of the runner is governed at the time of the pitch (where he was when the pitcher started the pitch). (Rule 7.10*a* —Any runner shall be called out on appeal when after a fly ball is caught, he fails to retouch his *original* base before he or the base is tagged.)

Got all the answers right? Terrific! Let's go on to the next inning.

SECOND INNING

1. The Tampico Stogies and Dothan Cardinals are tied in the bottom of the thirteenth inning with the bases loaded and Joe Louis Brown at the plate with two outs. Since the game is being played in Tampico, Brown has to be the final batter of the inning whether he reaches base or makes an out. Should the following batter, Stud Cantrell in this case, be forced to be in the on-deck circle in this situation or can he remain in the dugout with a pair of binoculars spying Dixie Lee Boxx in a third base box seat? If he fails to get in the on-deck circle do you warn him to go there and threaten to eject him from the game if he doesn't? (Or do you borrow the binoculars?) It's your call.

2. The Boston Braves are winning a laugher when their manager, Judge Emil Fuchs, decides to pull his regulars out of the lineup. But then the game gets much closer and Fuchs uses his entire bullpen to preserve what is now a slim lead, but it is to no avail. Finally, the Braves have a one-run lead in the top of the ninth inning when their backup shortstop takes a bad hop to the face and breaks his nose. The shortstop is unable to continue and the Braves are down to eight players. Do you allow them to play with eight players or forfeit the game to the visitors? It's your call.

3. The Colts are playing at Minnesota's Hubert H. Humphrey Metrodome and they trail the Twins by two runs in the last inning when right fielder Jaime Jan Orguyo van der Pijpers steps to the plate and rips a long high drive toward the outfield wall. The ball is obviously going to be a tape-measure homer before it smacks a speaker suspended from the ceiling and comes down in fair territory, where it is caught by an outfielder. Is it a ground-rule double, a home run or an out? It's your call.

4. Arsenic O'Reilly has a terrible move to first base, but he is sure the runner on first will try to steal on the next pitch. He decides he has no chance to pick the runner off first and doesn't want to call for a pitchout because he is already behind in the count to the hitter. O'Reilly has a brainstorm and decides to take a stretch, fire the ball to third and let the third baseman catch the runner stealing, even though third base is unoccupied at the time. Third baseman Oilcan Flynn is surprised by O'Reilly's throw but recovers in time to catch it and relay the ball to second baseman Bad News Galloway for the tag on the sliding runner. Should the runner be called out, or is the play described an illegal pickoff play? It's your call.

5. Rickey Sparks is brought in to relieve in a game for the Holyoke Redwings. He throws two pitches to the batter and the count goes to 2–0. The manager realizes his team cannot afford a walk in this situation and calls time-out to confer with Sparks. Sparks throws ball three on the next pitch and the angry manager sprints from the dugout to yank him out of the game, yet it is still the first batter he has faced. May the manager call for another reliever? Does Sparks have to stay in the game? Do you eject the manager for making an illegal visit to the mound? It's your call.

6. Moe Solomon, "the Rabbi of Swat," rips a ball to the left–center field gap and takes off for first base. But he steps on the plate in the

process. Should Solomon be called out for touching the bases out of the legal order, or should that be allowed on a base hit? It's your call.

7. Ellis "Old Folks" Kinder is in uniform and is scheduled to pitch tomorrow's game. As is the practice with his team, he is assigned to keep the chart of pitches tonight. Kinder decides he wants to sit in the stands behind home plate so he can see the pitches better. Would you allow this? It's your call.

8. Stinky Davis singles with no outs and is followed by Noodles Zupo, who cracks a home run on the first pitch. Davis, admiring Zupo's handiwork, misses second base. When a new ball is put in play the pitcher appeals the play at second base. Davis is out, but what do you do with Zupo? Is he out for passing the last legally touched base by Davis? Do you send him back to first base, or do you count his home run? It's your call.

9. Hog Durham drills a long home run with the bases loaded and two outs in the bottom of the ninth. The grand slam would give the Arkansas Reds a one-run victory. Julius Common Deer, who is the runner at second, stands on the bag watching the mammoth shot. Jefferson Mundy, who is on first base, begins tearing around the bases because he realizes he may have to score the tying run on a close play if the ball doesn't go out of the park. Mundy passes Deer at second base before Rainbow Smith can score from third base. What do you call? It's your call.

10. Ezra Dean reaches first on a base on balls for the Iowa Baseball Confederacy and is a big threat to steal second base in the late innings of a close game. The opposing catcher calls for a pitchout on the first pitch and, sure enough, Dean is stealing. The catcher, however, jumped out from the catcher's box behind the plate to take the pitchout while the pitcher was still in his delivery. Is this a catcher's balk and should Dean be awarded second base automatically? It's your call.

Two innings gone already! Check your second-inning answers on the following pages.

SECOND INNING ANSWERS

1. The next proper batter is required to be in the on-deck circle.

2. Forfeit the game. (Rule 1.01—Baseball is a game between two teams of nine players each. Rule 4.17—A game shall be forfeited to

the opposing team when a team is unable or refuses to place nine players on the field.)

3. Out. Situations such as this are determined before the game starts. Ground rules are made by the home team manager. (Rule 3.13 —The manager of the home team shall present to the umpire in chief and the opposing manager any ground rules he thinks necessary covering the overflow of spectators upon the playing field, batted or thrown balls into such overflow or any other contingencies.) In Minnesota, if a ball hits the roof or a speaker in fair territory and is caught by a fielder, the batter is out and base runners advance at their own risk.

4. Balk. (Rule 8.05d—A balk is called when there is a runner or runners on base, if the pitcher, while touching the rubber, throws or fakes a throw to an unoccupied base, except for the purpose of making a play at that unoccupied base.)

5. As the umpire, you make every effort to stop the manager from getting to the mound. He may not make a second trip while the same batter is at bat. In addition, as this is the first batter Sparks has faced, he must pitch one complete at-bat or retire the side before he can be removed. If the manager gets to the mound he will be ejected. Sparks will complete the necessary at-bat and then he will be removed from the game because of his manager's second trip. (Rule 8.06a, b, c and d and Rule 3.05b and c.)

6. Base hit, Solomon has done nothing illegal. Rule 7.02—in advancing, a runner shall touch first, second, third and home in order. But, budding umpires, don't be too technical. In situations such as this, common sense and fair play dictate that the runner has done nothing illegal.

7. Get Kinder out of there with his uniform on. If he changes into street clothes he may sit behind the plate. (Rule 3.09—Players in uniform shall not address or mingle with spectators nor sit in the stands before, during or after a game.)

8. Zupo scores, Davis is out for missing second. If there had been two outs, no runs would score because the base missed was a force out. Also, no following runs score if the missed base is the third out. (Rule 7.12—Unless two are out, the status of a following runner is not affected by a preceding runner's failure to touch or retouch a base. If upon appeal, the preceding runner is the third out, no runners following him shall score. If such third out is the result of a force play, neither preceding nor following runners shall score.)

9. No runs score. The third out occurs the moment Mundy passes Deer. If Smith had touched the plate before Mundy passed Deer, his run would count, but since he didn't, get ready for a big argument. (Rule 4.09a—One run shall be scored each time a runner legally advances to and touches first, second, third and home base before three men are put out to end an inning.)

10. No balk, allow the play to continue. (Rule 4.03a—The catcher may station himself directly back of the plate. He may leave his position at any time to catch a pitch or make a play, except that when the batter is being given an intentional base on balls, the catcher must stand with both feet within the lines of the catcher's box until the ball leaves the pitcher's hand.)

Don't forget to keep score of your answers for each inning.

THIRD INNING

1. Light-hitting Jack "Sour Mash" Daniels is at bat with one ball and two strikes on him. The bases are empty and there are no outs with Lynchburg trailing by one run in the bottom of the ninth. The pitcher uncorks a wild pitch which sails ten feet over Daniels's head. Daniels thinks quickly and swings at the wild pitch and reaches first base easily. Do you allow Daniels first base, or do you call the pitch a ball since he swung at the bad pitch to intentionally reach on a strike-out? It's your call.

2. Buddy Budlong is batting and he squares around to bunt but the pitch is wide. During his aborted bunt attempt, he steps on the plate. Budlong makes no contact with the ball, so should this be called just a strike or is he out for stepping on the plate while trying to make contact? It's your call.

3. Runners on first and second base with two outs. The New York Mammoths' Bruce Pearson loops a fly over the first baseman's head and it falls in for a Texas League hit. The runner on second comes around to score and after he crosses the plate, players on the other team tell him the ball fell foul. The runner starts walking back toward third and the coach there sends him back home. By this time the outfielder has retrieved the ball and has relayed it to the catcher who is waiting on the runner when he comes in, and the catcher easily tags him. Should the run count or did the runner give it up when he attempted to return to third base? It's your call.

4. A runner on first base gets fooled back to the bag as a pitcher delivers the ball to the plate. The lefthanded batter drills a hard grounder down the first base line and it hits the runner who has slid back into the bag. The runner is on the bag when he gets hit. Is the runner safe or out? What do you do with the batter? It's your call.

5. Casey is at the bat and the Mudville nine need a base runner desperately in the bottom of the ninth inning. The mighty Casey does not strike out this time, but instead smacks a hard grounder toward shortstop. In the process the bat is broken in half and the top half is headed in the same direction as the ball. The shortstop cannot make a play on the grounder because he is too busy dodging the bat. Do you allow Casey the hit, or call him out because his broken bat interfered with the play. Your decision may decide whether there will be any joy in Mudville that night. It's your call.

6. Harry "the Horse" Danning is on second base. Leaky Fausett is on first with two outs and a full count on Brains Padden. Danning and Fausett break before the pitch, but Louisville's reliever, Rubberlegs Miller, steps toward third base out of the stretch and throws the ball there to catch Danning sliding in. Should Danning be called out or is it a balk on Miller for making a pickoff move to an unoccupied base? It's your call.

7. Two runners on with two outs in the bottom of the ninth. The visitors are leading 6–4. The home team batter triples and both runners score. Time is called when the ball is thrown back to the infield. The third baseman calls for the ball, saying the second runner missed third base on his way to scoring the tying run. While the pitcher prepares to throw to third, the runner who had tripled breaks for home and is easily thrown out. Can the visiting team still appeal the runner missing the bag? Or does the inning end with the score tied because the third out was made on the play at home? It's your call.

8. Fats Berger steps to the plate and hits a grounder toward third base. The bat slips out of Berger's hands and hits the third baseman in the shins, making it impossible for him to make a play on Berger at first. Should Berger be allowed to stay on first because his bat had eyes on it or is he out for interfering with the play? It's your call.

9. Washington's Jesse "The Crab" Burkett is on second base with no outs and no one else on when Matches Kilroy hits a sinking line drive to right field. Burkett takes off thinking it will drop in for a hit, but has to retreat when the right fielder makes a great catch. Burkett

slides safely back into second, but overslides the base. The second baseman has the ball, so Burkett decides to now take off for first base and makes it with a beautiful hook slide around the first baseman's tag. Is Burkett safe at first or out for running the bases in the wrong direction? It's your call.

10. Bob "Death to Flying Things" Ferguson is on third base when Gilly Bigelow steps to the plate. Ferguson notices the pitcher has a long motion and decides to steal home. Bigelow doesn't realize Ferguson is coming and he swings at the pitch. The opposing catcher has stepped up on home plate to try and tag Ferguson. Bigelow's bat hits the catcher. Has the catcher interfered with Bigelow or has Bigelow interfered with the catcher's right to make a play at home? It's your call.

The third-inning answers follow.

THIRD INNING ANSWERS

1. In appreciation of Danials's ability to think that quickly, you may allow the play to stand. (Rule 5.03—The pitcher shall deliver the pitch to the batter who may elect to strike the ball, or who may not offer at it, as he chooses. Rule 6.09b—The batter becomes a runner when the third strike called by the umpire is not caught, provided first base is unoccupied.) If Daniels had been a little slow and swung after the ball was clearly at the backstop, you may not judge this as a swing at the pitch. In every case, you should rule with common sense and fair play in mind.

2. No, he is not out. He would be out, however, if he made contact with the ball regardless of whether the ball went fair or foul. (Rule 6.06a—The batter is out for illegal action when he hits a ball with one or both feet on the ground entirely outside the batter's box.) As long as no contact was made, the pitch is a ball or strike depending on whether or not it's in the strike zone.

3. The run counts. A run legally scored cannot be nullified if the runner legally touched first, second, third and home. (Rule 5.06—When a batter becomes a runner and touches all bases legally he shall score one run for his team.) A run legally scored cannot be nullified by subsequent action of the runner, such as, but not limited to, an effort to return to third in belief that he had left the base before a caught fly ball.

4. The runner is out. The base does not protect the runner from a batted ball. (Rule 7.08*f*—A runner is out when he is touched by a fair ball in fair territory before the ball has been touched or passed by an infielder.) The batter receives credit for a base hit, and is awarded first base.

5. No interference on a broken bat. However, if he had thrown a whole bat, intentionally or not, Casey would have been out. (Rule 6.05*h*—If a bat breaks and part of it is in fair territory and is hit by a batted ball or part of it hits a runner or fielder, play shall continue and no interference called. If a whole bat is thrown into fair territory and interferes with a defensive player attempting to make a play, interference shall be called, whether intentional or not.)

6. Legal play. (Rule 8.05*d*—A balk is called when there is a runner or runners on base, if the pitcher, while touching the rubber, throws or fakes a throw to an unoccupied base, except for the purpose of making a play at that unoccupied base.) Miller worked within the rules because he was making a play at third.

7. No appeal allowed, tie score. (Rule 7.10*d*—Any appeal under this rule must be made before the next pitch or play or attempted play.)

8. Interference, Berger is out. Intent is not the question here; Berger is out whether or not he intended to interfere. (Rule 6.05*h*—If a whole bat is thrown into fair territory and interferes with a defensive player attempting to make a play, interference shall be called whether intentional or not.)

9. Burkett is out. (Rule 7.08*i*—Any runner is out when after he has acquired legal possession of a base he runs the bases in reverse order for the purpose of confusing the defense.) This does not hold true for a runner decoyed into returning to a previously occupied base. An example of this is when a runner on first steals second, but is decoyed into returning to first by tricky infielders. He may be tagged out en route to returning to first, but once he reaches his previously occupied base he is safe.

10. The catcher has interfered. Score the run and give Bigelow first base on catcher's interference. (Rule 6.08*c*—The batter becomes a runner and is entitled to first base without liability to be put out when the catcher or any infielder interferes with him. The runner scores because of Rule 7.04*d*—Each runner, other than the batter, may without liability to be put out, advance one base while he is attempting to steal

a base, if the batter is interfered with by the catcher or any other fielder.)

It's time again to check those answers and your umpiring skills.

FOURTH INNING

1. Henry Wiggen is at the plate. On a two-strike pitch, Wiggen foul tips the ball. Bruce Pearson, the catcher, catches the ball after it caroms off his mask but before it hits the ground. Is Wiggen out, or is it just a foul ball since Pearson did not catch it directly in his glove? It's your call.

2. Roy Hobbs has been out with Mimi a little too late one night and when he rushes to the ballpark the next day, he forgets to take most of his equipment. Hobbs's teammates are tired of covering for their slumping slugger and decide they are not going to lend Hobbs a glove or a hat. The equipment manager is nowhere to be found. Hobbs takes his position in right field without his hat or glove. Do you let him play? It's your call.

3. It is late in a long, dreary game that has been stalled repeatedly by rain delays. With the bases loaded and an 0–2 count on the batter, the catcher, Blackie Mancuso, sets up for a waste pitch way out of the strike zone. So far, in fact, that he is entirely out of the catcher's box. The only problem is the catcher's box has been erased from the action around the plate and the bad weather. Do you call time and have a new catcher's box drawn in? Do you warn the catcher he is pushing the boundaries of the now imaginary box? Do you call a balk because he is out of the box? Do you ignore it and call anything close to the strike zone a strike? Or do you do nothing at all? It's your call.

4. Bases are loaded with one out in the bottom of the ninth inning of a tie game. The fielding team pulls everyone in to cut down the run at the plate and the batter drives the ball over the center fielder's head. The runner on third scores easily, but the rest of the runners retire to their dugout to prepare for a party after the game, without advancing a base. The center fielder retrieves the ball and on his way to the first base dugout he steps on second and first with the ball in hand. Double play? Do you count the run since everybody else has left the field? It's your call.

5. Socks Perry is the runner on first base and he makes a break to steal second. The opposing pitcher panics and makes a horrible move to throw the ball to first base. The only thing worse than the pitcher's move is his throw, which winds up in the right field bullpen. Perry proceeds to round the bases. Do you allow the run or do you put the runner back on second and just award him one base for the balk? It's your call.

6. Horse Belly Sargent hits a gapper and goes for a triple. When Sargent lumbers into third base, he and the third baseman collide. The ball goes one way and the players go the other. Sargent's helmet is knocked off in the collision. The third baseman finds the ball and attempts to tag Sargent as he dives back toward the bag. Sargent grabs his helmet, lunges toward the bag and reaches around the tag with his helmet and holds it to the base. Meanwhile, the third baseman tags Sargent on the arm. Is Sargent safe or out because he used the helmet? It's your call.

7. Dashing Dan Costello rips a ferocious line drive up the middle which hits the pitcher's rubber on the line and rebounds back to the catcher behind the plate on the fly. The catcher calmly fields the ball and throws the ball to first to beat the stunned Costello. Is Costello out? It's your call.

8. Hooks Cotter is on third with two outs and Klondike Douglass at the plate with an 0–2 count. The pitcher delivers a sharp breaking ball in the dirt. Douglass appears to check his swing and the catcher cannot hang onto the pitch, which gets by to the backstop. An alert Cotter scores. The catcher then asks for an appeal on the checked swing and the third-base umpire rules that Douglass did indeed swing. The catcher tags Douglass for the third out. Do you count the run? It's your call.

9. Bases are empty and the batter pops up to the first baseman. The first baseman touches the ball in fair territory, but bobbles the ball. The ball gets away from the first baseman and hits the batter, who is racing for first base, in foul territory. The second baseman, who has come over to back up the play, catches the ball after it caroms off of the runner, but before it touches the ground. Is the batter out, safe or is this a foul ball? It's your call.

10. Buttercup Dickerson is fooled on a bad pitch and tries to check his swing to avoid striking out. The pitch gets away from the catcher and Dickerson hoofs it for first base and reaches safely. The plate

umpire calls the pitch a ball. You are the first base umpire and Dickerson asks you to appeal the call, hoping to get aboard the easy way. Do you pass judgment over whether the batter swung at the pitch or do you send Dickerson back to bat? It's your call.

Check yourself against the fourth inning answers. You should be getting the hang of this by now.

FOURTH INNING ANSWERS

1. This call depends on whether or not the ball hit the catcher's hand or glove first. (Rule 2.00—A *foul tip* is a batted ball that goes directly from the bat to the catcher's glove or hand and is legally caught. It is not a foul tip unless caught and any foul tip caught is a strike, and the ball is in play. It is not a catch if it is a rebound, such as off the mask or protection, unless it has first touched hand or mitt.) If it touched hand or mitt first, Wiggin is out.

2. Roy may play without a glove (Rule 1.14—A fielder may use a leather glove, but does not have to use one). The hat, however, is a different story. (Rule 1.11—All players on a team shall wear uniforms identical in color, trim and style, and all players' uniforms shall include minimal six-inch numbers on their backs. . . . No player whose uniform does not conform to that of his teammates shall be permitted to participate in a game.)

3. None of the above. This is a legal play by the catcher. In this situation the catcher's box does not come into play. The catcher may leave the box at any time to catch a pitch or make a play. It is not a balk to leave the catcher's box before the pitcher releases the ball except on an intentional walk. (Rule 4.03a—The catcher shall station himself directly back of the plate. He may leave his position at any time to catch a pitch or make a play except when the batter is being given an intentional walk.)

4. This is a tough one. The runners are forced to touch the next base because these are force plays. But, on an inning-ending play, Rule 7.10 kicks in—Any appeal under this rule must be made before the next pitch or play or attempted play. If the violation occurs during a play which ends a half-inning, the appeal must be made before the defensive team leaves the field. . . . For the purpose of this rule the defensive team has "left the field" when the pitcher and all infielders

have left fair territory on their way to the bench or clubhouse. If all the infielders have left, the appeal is too late.

5. Let the runner proceed. If a balk was called, use Rule 8.05 (In cases where a pitcher balks and throws wild, either to a base or to home plate, a runner or runners may advance beyond the base to which he was entitled at his own risk.)

6. As far as our panel of experts can tell, this one isn't covered in the rulebook. The consensus is, call Sargent out, since he should not be allowed to gain an advantage by using detached equipment. (Rule 9.01c—Each umpire has the authority to rule on any point not specifically covered in the rules.)

7. It depends on where the ball was touched by a fielder. When the ball hit the rubber it was no longer in flight, so the batter is not out on the catch. As with any batted ball, if the fielder, in this case the catcher, touched the ball while the ball was on or over fair territory then it is a fair ball and the play stands. If the catcher touches the ball while the ball is over foul territory it is a foul ball. It is not the position of the catcher's feet or body, but the position of the ball when touched (Rule 2.00).

8. The run does not count. (Rule 4.09a—One run shall be scored each time a runner legally advances to and touches first, second, third and home before three men are put out to end the inning. Exception: A run is not scored if the runner advances to home base during a play in which the third out is made by the batter-runner before he touches first base.)

9. Fair ball. No catch. The first baseman touched the ball while it was over fair territory. (Rule 2.00—A *catch* is the act of the fielder in getting a secure possession in his hand or glove of a ball in flight and firmly holding it, providing he does not use his cap, protector, pocket or any other part of his uniform in getting possession. It is not a catch, however, if simultaneously or immediately following his contact with the ball he collides with a player or with a wall, or if he falls down, and as a result of such collisions or falling, drops the ball. It is not a catch if a fielder touches a fly ball which then hits a member of the offensive team or an umpire and then is caught by another defensive player.)

10. Only the defense may ask for an appeal. Dickerson and his teammates are the offense. The call of ball must stand. (Rule 2.00— An *appeal* is the act of a fielder in claiming violation by the offense.)

Turn to the back of the book again to find the next stop in your umpiring career. Are you moving up faster than the thermometer in July or have you had more umpiring setbacks than there are stems in a pouch of bad chewing tobacco?

FIFTH INNING

1. The Mudville nine is ahead 4–0 after six innings and Casey comes to bat in the top of the seventh and belts a three-run homer. After Casey completes his jaunt around the bases, a downpour of rain comes and rains out the game. Is the final score 7–0 or does the score revert back to the last completed inning and 4–0, leaving the mighty Casey holding the bag? It's your call.

2. A runner is on first base when the ball is hit over the left fielder's head. The second baseman waltzes over toward the bag as the runner on first begins to round second and the two collide. The ball takes a funny bounce and rolls around the left field corner. The runner is able to get up and advance to third, but decides not to attempt to score as the ball comes in to the relay man. Do you allow the runner to score or do you just allow him one base for obstruction on the second baseman? It's your call.

3. Washington's Skip Hatten is on first base and takes off on a hit-and-run play with Jason Cornell at the plate. The pitch is outside. Cornell lunges for the ball and the bat slips out of his hands and toward second base. The catcher on the opposing team throws the ball to second in an attempt to catch Hatten stealing, but the ball hits the bat in midair and sails into center field. Hatten advances to third on the overthrow. Do you allow Hatten to stay at third, put him back at second or call interference on Cornell? It's your call.

4. Bloody Jake Evans fades back on a deep fly ball and leaps at the fence to catch the long drive. He makes the stab, but as he does, he falls over the fence in fair territory. Home run or out? It's your call.

5. Harvard Eddie Grant of the Minneapolis Millers gets caught in a rundown between third and home. The catcher chases Grant back toward third base and throws the ball to the third baseman. As the catcher throws the ball he slips and falls in the baseline. Grant turns to run toward home and trips on the catcher and is tagged by the third baseman. The catcher's fall was accidental and he was not blocking

the base path intentionally. Do you call Grant out or do you award the Millers a run because of the obstruction? It's your call.

6. With a runner on first base and one out, the ball is popped-up down the third-base line near the dugout. The Iowa Baseball Confederacy's Oilcan Flynn rushes over from his third-base position and catches the ball in fair territory. Flynn's momentum carries him into the dugout. Do you allow the runner on first an extra base because Flynn carried the ball out of play, make him stay put, or allow him to advance at his own risk? It's your call.

7. Hughie "Ee-Yah" Jennings's Detroit Tigers are having a particularly rough time and he's been on your back all day. The Tigers trail 11–2 in the eighth inning when Jennings comes to the plate. You are the first-base umpire. Jennings hits a solo home run and as he rounds first base he lets loose with some choice profane comments about your heritage. He's gotta go, so you toss him out of the game right then and there. But even though you've yanked him between first and second base, he completes the circuit, touching third and home. Does the run still count? It's your call.

8. Bases are loaded with one out in the bottom of the ninth of a tie game. Steady Pete Meegan walks the batter, who peels off to join the postgame celebration before he reaches first base. Do you allow the runner from third to score the winning run, or should you call the batter out and send the runners back to their bases since the hitter didn't reach first to force them around the bases? It's your call.

9. Joe Hardy is a nervous rookie in class A ball. He hits a looping fly ball to short right field that falls in. Hardy, not wanting anybody else to use his precious bat, carries it with him as he slides safely in for a double. Do you let the double stand or do you send Hardy and his precious bat back to the dugout? It's your call.

10. You've made it to the big time and you're umpiring a World Series game. Cincinnati leads the Yankees by four runs in the bottom of the eighth inning when New York rallies for three runs and has the bases loaded. The score is now 6–5, there are still no outs, and a heavy rain begins to fall. Before you and your crew can stop the game a Yankee hitter singles and knocks in two runs to give New York the lead. The rain falls even harder and the game is stopped with still no outs in the bottom of the eighth. The game is washed out. Do the Yankees, who are leading 7–6, win or do you revert back to the last completed inning and award the Reds a 6–2 victory? It's your call.

For the fifth inning answers, keep reading. Don't cheat, though. This is now a legal game, and it counts in the standings.

FIFTH INNING ANSWERS

1. Give Casey his round-tripper. The final score should be 7–0, since the home run did not affect the outcome of the game. The reverting back rule was removed in 1980. There are no reverting back situations. If, however, Mudville had been trailing and Casey's homer gave his team the lead, the game would be suspended at that point and completed at a later date. If this last situation had occurred in the bottom of the inning, the game would be over.

2. Obstruction occurred at second base. The runner should score. (Rule 7.06b—If no play is being made on the obstructed runner, the play shall proceed until no further action is possible. The umpire shall then call time-out and impose such penalties, if any, that in his judgment will nullify the act of obstruction.

3. Call interference, the batter is out. Runners return to their original bases. It does not matter whether the batter's act of throwing the bat was unintentional or not. (Rule 6.06c—The batter is out when he interferes with the catcher's fielding or throwing by stepping out of the batter's box or making any other movement that hinders the catcher's play at home base. Rule 6.05h—If a whole bat is thrown into fair territory and interferes with a defensive player attempting to make a play, interference shall be called whether intentional or not.)

4. Out. (Rule 2.00—A *catch* is the act of a fielder in getting secure possession in his hand or glove of a ball in flight and firmly holding it. . . . A fielder may reach over a fence, railing, rope or other line of demarcation to make a catch. He may jump on top of a railing or canvas even if they are in foul ground.) Runners on base would advance one base. (Rule 7.04c—If the fielder or catcher, after having made a legal catch, should fall into a stand or among spectators or into the dugout after making a legal catch, or fall while in the dugout after making a legal catch, the ball is dead and runners advance one base without liability to be put out.)

5. Obstruction, score the run, intent is not the question. (Rule 7.06a—If a play is being made on the obstructed runner, such as a rundown, or if the batter-runner is obstructed before he touches first base, the ball is dead and all runners shall advance, without liability

to be put out, to the bases they would have reached, in the umpire's judgment, had there been no obstruction. The obstructed runner shall be awarded at least one base beyond the base he last legally touched before the obstruction.)

6. The ball is in play, everyone is at their own peril. The dugout is only out of play on a throw. In professional baseball, players may enter the dugout to make a catch. If the player remains standing the ball is alive and in play. If, after making the catch, the fielder falls in the dugout then all runners would advance one base. This holds true for all dead-ball areas (i.e., bullpens, etc.). You may catch and carry the ball into these areas and the ball remains alive. But, if the fielder falls, then the ball is dead. (Rule 5.10*f*—When a fielder after making a catch steps into a bench, but does not fall, the ball is in play and runners may advance at their own peril.)

7. Even though you have ejected him immediately, Jennings will be allowed to complete the play (in this case, round the bases). When the play is completed he is done for the day. (Rule 9.01*d*—If an umpire disqualifies a player while a play is in progress, the disqualification shall not take effect until no further action is possible in that play.)

8. Spoil the party! Declare the batter out and send the runner back to third. (Rule 6.08*a*—The batter is entitled to first base without liability to be put out provided he advances to and touches first base when four balls are called by the umpire. A batter who is entitled to first base because of a base on balls must go to first base and touch the base before other base runners are forced to advance. Rule 4.09*b* —When the winning run is scored in the last half-inning of a regulation game, or in the last half extra inning, as the result of a base on balls, hit batter, or other award of bases, with the bases full which forces the runner on third to advance, the umpire shall not declare the game ended until the runner forced to advance from third has touched home *and* the batter-runner has touched first base.)

9. Hardy is OK, albeit weird. Give him a double. Fall back on Rule 9.01*c*—there is no rule stating the batter-runner cannot carry the bat. If in your judgment it did not hinder, confuse or impede the defense, Hardy is OK.

10. As we said in answer number 1 in this section, there is no longer any "reverting back." The Yanks would win this one 7–6. (Rule 4.11—The score of a regulation game is the total number of runs scored

by each team at the moment the game ends; 4.11*d*—A called game ends at the moment the umpire terminates play. *Exception:* If the game is called while an inning is in progress and before it is completed, the game becomes *suspended* if: (1) the visiting team scores one or more runs, in that half-inning, to tie the score and the home team has not taken the lead; (2) The visiting team has scored one or more runs to take the lead, in its half-inning, and the home team has not taken the lead.) The Yankees took the lead in its home half of the inning. They win.

So how's your career progressing? Record your score on the scoreboard.

SIXTH INNING

1. Rainbow Smith of the Arkansas Reds is on third base and Jeremiah Eversole tries a suicide squeeze to bring him home in a close game. Eversole gets the bunt down, but Smith doesn't get a good break from third. The bunt is rolling down the first-base line and as the first baseman tries to field it and make a play at home, Eversole plows him over. The first baseman is unable to make a play at either home or first base. Do you allow the run? Do you call Eversole out for interference? Do you call Smith out because Eversole interfered? Are both runners out? It's your call.

2. With the bases loaded and two outs, Warren "Buddy" Budlong hurries home with the potential tying run as Jason Cornell hits a sharp grounder in the hole between third and shortstop. The third baseman makes a diving stop and scrambles up and attempts to tag Opie Wright, the runner coming in from second. Wright retreats to second base and the third baseman flips the ball to the shortstop who makes the tag. In the meantime, Budlong has crossed the plate before the tag was made. Do you count the run since it scored before the tag and since the third baseman chose not to make the force play at third? It's your call.

3. The Butte Copper Kings have Sam Mejias on first base when Heine Meine, a.k.a. "The Count of Luxemburg," fouls a pitch off. Pocatello pitcher Porky Odom receives a new ball from the umpire and as he is walking up the pitcher's mound he notices that Mejias has retouched and is already taking a big lead. Odom quickly fires over and picks Mejias off. Is Mejias out? It's your call.

4. Cincinnati leads the Dodgers by three runs in the top of the ninth in a game at Riverfront Stadium. The Dodgers have bases loaded when Kirk Gibson singles to right field. Paul O'Neill's throw to the plate is high and gets by catcher Bo Diaz. Schottzie, Reds owner Marge Schott's Saint Bernard, leaps from her first-base box seat and fetches the ball. Like any good dog, Schottzie jumps over the railing and takes the ball to Schott. The owner then fires the ball back to Diaz in time for him to tag the incoming runner, who started on first base. How many runs do you allow and is the runner Diaz tagged out? It's your call.

5. Dirty Al Gallagher hits a long, high drive that appears to be heading out of the park. A Chicago outfielder scales the wall, however, and pulls himself up onto the scoreboard where he makes the catch, balancing himself on top of the wall and leaning on the scoreboard. Does Gallagher touch them all or beat a hasty retreat to the dugout and tip his hat to the acrobatic outfielder? It's your call.

6. E.T.A. Whitaker is on third base and is taking his lead in foul territory when Scrappy "Dirtbrain" Hawthorn hits a wicked grounder in Whitaker's direction. Whitaker retreats toward the bag. When he reaches the base, the ball strikes him and bounds into foul territory. Fair ball, foul ball, is the runner on third out? What about the batter? It's your call.

7. An opposing runner attempts to steal second base against the Toledo Mud Hens. Catcher Bill Nahorodny realizes he has no chance to catch the runner so he attempts a trick play by throwing a pop-up to the second baseman, Iron Hands Hiller. The shortstop points up at the ball and calls for Hiller to throw the ball to first base to complete their decoyed double-play. The confused baserunner slides safely into second base, but gets up when he sees the ball in the air and retreats toward first base. Hiller is laughing so hard that his throw is wide and the runner makes it back to first safely. Is this a legal decoy? Should the runner be called out for running the bases backward after already reaching second safely? It's your call.

8. A batter hits a ball to right center field and outfielders Bobo Breazeale and Shaun Fitzmaurice converge on it. Breazeale makes the catch as the two collide and the force of the collision knocks the glove off of Breazeale's hand. The ball, however, stays put in the glove as it falls to the ground. Breazeale and Fitzmaurice are out—cold, that is. But is the batter out, or can he go for as many bases as he can get? It's your call—and then call for the trainers and smelling salts.

9. Runners on first and second with no outs. Henry Pulvermacher grounds the ball to third base where the third sacker fields the ball and attempts to tag the runner coming toward him. The runner retreats to second to avoid the tag and the third baseman then throws the ball there and the second baseman tags the bag for the force out on the runner from first, but cannot make the tag on the retreating runner. Is the runner who began on second out for running the bases in the wrong direction or for failing to advance on a force play, or is his move legal since the force has been removed? It's your call.

10. White Wings Tebeau hits a sharp line drive up the middle. But the ball strikes the pitcher's shoe and deflects toward the first-base line and hits Tebeau as he is running in fair territory toward first base. Is Tebeau out for being hit with the ball in fair territory? It's your call.

Got your answers all figured out? Don't dawdle—remember that split-second time limit real umpires have to face. Turn to the sixth inning answers, and watch out for the managers charging out to kick dirt on you!

SIXTH INNING ANSWERS

1. Interference. The batter is out. If in your judgment the batter deliberately caused interference to break up a double play, you may call out both the batter and the runner closest to home. (Rule 7.08*b* —A runner is out when he hinders a fielder attempting to make a play on a batted ball, whether intentional or not. Rule 7.09*h*—If in the judgment of the umpire, a batter-runner willfully and deliberately interferes with a batted ball or a fielder in the act of fielding a batted ball, with the obvious intent to break up a double play, the ball is dead; the umpire shall call the batter out for interference, and shall also call out the runner who had advanced closest to home plate regardless where the double play might have been possible.)

2. No run scores. Even though they tagged the runner it was still a force play. (Rule 2.00—A *force play* is a play where a runner legally loses his right to occupy a base by reason of the batter becoming the runner. Rule 4.09*a*—*Exception:* A run is not scored during a play in which the third out is made by any runner being forced out.)

3. No, Majias is OK. (Rule 5.02—After the umpire calls "play" the ball is alive and in play until for legal cause—in this case, a foul ball —or at the umpire's call of "time" suspending play, the ball becomes

dead. While the ball is dead no player may be put out, no bases may be run and no runs may score.) The umpire amust acknowledge that the ball is in play, usually by pointing at the pitcher while the pitcher has possession of the new ball and is touching the pitcher's plate. (Rule 5.11—After the ball is dead, play shall be resumed when the pitcher takes his position on the pitcher's plate with a new ball or the same ball in his possession and the plate umpire calls "play").

4. This is spectator interference. You can't miss this one. Whatever the umpire does is correct. As the umpire, you try to determine what would have happened if Schottzie had kept her big mouth shut. You can put runners on the bases you believe they would have achieved. You could even call runners out if you felt the Reds' pitcher was backing up the play and would get them. (Rule 3.16—When there is spectator interference with any thrown or batted ball, the ball shall be dead at the moment of interference and the umpire shall impose such penalties as in his opinion will nullify the act of interference.)

5. Long fly out. Ball was caught in flight. (Rule 2.00 and Rule 5.10*f*.)

6. The position of the ball is the determining factor in this call. If the ball was in foul territory when the runner was struck by the ball it is foul. If the ball was over fair territory when it struck the runner, the runner is out. The base does not protect the runner when hit by a fair batted ball. (Rule 7.08*f*—Any runner is out when touched by a fair ball in fair territory before the ball has touched or passed an infielder.) If a fair ball, the runner is out and the batter is awarded first base and is credited with a base hit.

7. Yes, this would be a legal decoy. The runner is OK, however. (Rule 7.08*i*—If a runner touches an unoccupied base and then thinks the ball was caught or is decoyed into returning to the base he last touched, he may be put out running back to that base, but if he reaches the previously occupied base safely he cannot be put out while in contact with that base.)

8. No catch. Let the runner run. (Rule 2.00—A catch is the act of a fielder getting secure possession in his hand or glove and firmly holding it. It is not a catch, however, if simultaneously or immediately following his contact with the ball, he collides with a player, or wall, or he falls down, and as a result of such collision, drops the ball.)

9. Running move is legal! He's safe at second. (Rule 7.08*e*—Any runner is out when he fails to reach the next base before a fielder tags

him or the base, after he has been forced to advance by reason of the batter becoming a runner. However, if a following runner is put out on a force play, the force is removed and the runner must be tagged to be put out.)

10. No, fair ball, in play. (Rule 7.08*f*—The runner is out when he is touched by a fair ball *before* the ball has touched or passed an infielder.) For the purpose of this rule the pitcher is an infielder who has been touched with the ball.

Do you feel like you're working in the big leagues yet, or are you ready to turn in your umpiring gear for a used bicycle?

SEVENTH INNING

1. Bases are loaded, two outs. The runners are going with the pitch, which is ball four. The runner going to second base slides and goes past the bag. The alert catcher, Dimples Tate, makes a quick throw and the second baseman tags the runner before the runner from third crosses the plate. Do you allow the run or disallow it because the third out was made before the runner from third touched the plate? It's your call.

2. Arlie Tarbert is on third base with one out when the ball is hit deep to left field. The left fielder makes the catch after bobbling the ball for a couple of seconds. Tarbert tagged up and left the bag when the outfielder first touched the ball, but before he completed his catch. The defense appeals that he left too early. It's your call.

3. Sheriff Gainor hits a sharp line drive up the middle that pitcher Rhino Hitt catches on one bounce. The ball was hit so hard, however, that it gets wedged in the webbing of Hitt's glove and he can't get it out. Hitt gives up and throws his glove, with the ball still in it, to first baseman Boots Grantham, who catches the glove and its contents before Gainor reaches first base. Is this a legal putout and should you hand it—or glove it—to Hitt for fast thinking? Or should Gainor be given the base because two gloves are not necessarily better than one? It's your call.

4. Frank Joiner is on second base and John "Apples" Bagwell is on first with no outs. Narvel Adams lifts a pop fly to the infield, but the second baseman loses it in the sun and it takes one bounce and hits

Joiner as he stands on second base. Is Joiner out for interference and, if so, is this a double play since the batter has already been declared out on the infield fly rule? It's your call.

5. The Arkansas Reds have just completed the top of the third inning. As the home team comes to bat in the bottom of the third inning, the lights come on. Lefty Marks, the Reds' manager, protests to the umpires that they can't turn the lights on until the next inning because his team had to bat in the third inning without lights. Will Lefty's protest be upheld?

6. George "Old Wax Figger" Hemming is the victim of a practical joke by his teammates. In his last pitching stint he got hammered and the players ribbed him unmercifully about the shellacking. As a joke they painted his glove white. In his next turn in the rotation he still hadn't bought a new glove. He attempts to use his glove, which is still painted white. Do you allow him to use the glove or do you rule it would be too big a distraction for the batters? It's your call.

7. Razzle Dazzle Murphy breaks off a nasty two-strike curveball on Ding-a-Ling Clay and it bounces a foot in front of the plate. Ding-a-Ling is fooled on the pitch but somehow his mighty swing catches enough of it on the bounce to send it over the right center field fence. Home run or foul ball? It's your call.

8. You're having a rough game and you've already ejected three coaches and the manager from the home team. The team is down to only two more coaches and the acting manager decides he doesn't want to use any of his players as base coaches because he's afraid you might run them as well. So he doesn't send any base coaches out when his team hits in the bottom of the eighth. Do you allow the home team to bat since they are bringing the disadvantage upon themselves or do you insist the acting manager use base coaches? It's your call.

9. Cozy Dolan hits a fly ball down the right field line and the right fielder drifts under the ball in foul territory as the wind pushes it back toward fair ground. The right fielder, whose feet are both still in foul ground, does a circus act and can't hang on for the catch. The ball caroms off his glove, which is over fair territory, and bounces fair. Fair or foul? It's your call.

10. Grandma Murphy is called upon to sacrifice bunt Topsy Magoon over to second base. He squares to lay down the bunt but changes his mind and tries to pull back at the last instant. But Murphy is not quick enough and gets hit on the forearm with the pitch, which

101

comes in on the inside corner of the plate. Do you call him out for interference, give him first base, call the pitch a strike or simply call it a ball? It's your call.

SEVENTH INNING STRETCH

OK, everyone, let's get up and sing:

> Take me out to the ball game!
> Take me out with the crowd!
> Buy me some peanuts and Cracker Jack!
> I don't care if I ever get back!
> For let's root, root, root for the *umpire!*
> If he's* not right it's a shame!
> For it's *Hrike Hunn! Hrike hooo! Hrike hree! Yerrr outtt!*
> At the old ball game.

*Apologies to Pam Postema.

There. Wasn't that fun? Now, get yourself a tall cool one, swallow hard, and turn to the trusty seventh inning answers.

SEVENTH INNING ANSWERS

1. Believe it or not, *allow the run* and call the runner oversliding second base *out*. (Rule 7.04—Each runner, other than the batter, may without liability to be put out, advance one base when the batter's advance without liability to be put out forces the runner to vacate his base. A runner forced to advance without liability to be put out, such as when a walk forces the advance, may advance past the base to which he is entitled only at his own peril. If such runner, forced to advance, is put out for the third out before a preceding runner, also forced to advance, touches the plate, the run shall score.) The run would score on the theory that the run was forced home by the base on balls and that all the runners needed to do was proceed and touch the next base.

2. It's a catch and the runner is safe. He may tag up as soon as a defensive player touches the ball. (Rule 2.00—A catch is legal if the ball is finally held by any fielder, even though juggled, or held by another fielder before it touches the ground. Runners may leave their bases the instant the first fielder touches the ball.)

3. Out. The first baseman tagged first while having secure possession of the ball in his hand or glove. He also happened to have Hitt's

glove. (Rule 2.00—A *tag* is the action of a fielder in touching a base with his body while holding the ball securely and firmly in his hand or glove. While a fielder may not throw his glove *at* a batted or thrown ball, there is no restriction on tossing glove and ball together.)

4. No, the runner is not out. (Rule 7.08f—*Exception:* If a runner is touching his base when touched by an infield fly, he is not out, although the batter is out.) If it had not been declared an infield fly, then the runner is out.

5. No, the protest will not be allowed. Although it is common courtesy to try to turn the lights on at the top of an inning, the umpire may legally turn them on at any time. (Rule 4.14—The umpire-in-chief shall order the playing field lights turned on whenever, in his opinion, darkness makes further play in daylight hazardous.)

6. Of course he cannot use it, nor may a pitcher wear a gray glove. (Rule 1.15a—The pitcher's glove may not be white or gray.)

7. Clay can touch them all, it's a home run. (Rule 2.00—If the pitch touches the ground and bounces through the strike zone it is a ball. If such pitch touches a batter, he shall be awarded first base. If the batter swings at such a pitch after two strikes and misses, the ball cannot be caught. For the purposes of Rule 6.05, he must be tagged as on any dropped third strike. If the batter hits such a pitch, the ensuing action shall be the same as if he hit the ball in flight.)

8. Make him send out some base coaches and if he gripes too much run him, too. (Rule 4.05—The offensive team shall station two base coaches on the field during its turn at bat.)

9. The ball is fair. (Rule 2.00—A fair fly shall be judged according to the relative position of the ball and the foul line, including the foul pole, and not as to whether the fielder is in fair territory at the time he touches the ball.)

10. Stick up the right hand, because it's a strike. (Rule 2.00—A legal pitch that touches the batter in the strike zone is still a strike.)

Almost done! Time for that late inning rally!

EIGHTH INNING

1. Bootnose Hofmann is catching and there's a play at the plate. The runner slides around Hofmann's tag, but also misses the plate. Hofmann doesn't notice the runner missed home. When the runner reaches the dugout, the first baseman yells to Hofmann that the runner missed home. Hofmann runs into the dugout and begins tagging everybody in sight, but the runner sneaks out of the end of the dugout before he is tagged and bolts back toward home plate. Hofmann throws the ball to pitcher Coonskin Davis, who is now covering and the runner beats the throw. Is the runner safe and do you score the run, or is he out when the team on the field begins the appeal process while he has already retired to the dugout? It's your call.

2. The Beaumont Golden Gators have the bases loaded with two outs with Pug Bennett on third base and Nig Grabowski on first. The runners leave with the pitch and the ball is grounded to second base. The second baseman attempts to tag Grabowski for the third out of the inning, but misses him as Grabowski goes out of the base path. Grabowski is out, but not before the speedy Bennett has crossed the plate. Do you count the run?

3. Hondo Hollmig leads off the inning for the Bur-Gra Pirates with a single. Beauty Bancroft then follows him in the lineup with a single to right on a perfectly executed hit-and-run play. Hollmig, however, steps right over second base on his way to third base. The opposing right fielder throws the ball into second base and the shortstop takes the relay while standing on the second base bag. Do you call the force out on Hollmig since he never touched second base, or does the defense have to appeal the play? It's your call.

4. Eddie Collins is on third base, Chick Gandil is on first with one out. Shoeless Joe Jackson hits a deep drive to the left center field gap, but the ball is caught. Collins tags and easily scores from third, but Gandil, thinking the ball was going to drop, is caught between second and third when the catch is made. Gandil scrambles and tries to get back to first base, but the throw just beats him for the third out. Collins has already crossed the plate. Do you count the run or not? It's your call.

5. Crash Davis drives an inside fastball deep over the left field fence to break a scoreless tie in the thirteenth inning. As Davis rounds first base, he looks up to admire his long shot and twists his ankle badly on the base. Davis falls to the ground in pain and cannot get up to

continue his trip around the bases. Can Davis's team insert a pinch runner to complete the round-tripper or do you call him out since he left the base path as he was writhing in pain from the sprained ankle? It's your call.

6. The Lodi Crushers have the bases loaded and two outs when their cleanup hitter strikes out. Victorville catcher Bear Gile can't hang onto the pitch, however, and all the runners try to move up a base. Gile finds the ball and instead of risking a throw to first base, steps on home plate to force the runner there. Is this a legal play? Can Gile force somebody at home on a strikeout? It's your call.

7. Jamie Don Weeks is on third base with one out in the bottom of the ninth of a tie game. Stud Cantrell hits a long fly ball down the right field line in foul territory. Weeks will certainly score on the sacrifice fly if the ball is caught, but the outfielder never gets a chance to make the play because a fan reaches over the right field railing and catches the ball with a fishnet. It's a clear case of interference, but what do you do with Weeks on third base? Does he score the winning run? It's your call.

8. Bases are loaded with one out in the bottom of the ninth inning of a tie game. You're working a two-man crew so you are stationed behind the pitcher between first and second. Orville Swan hits a blue darter line drive, which hits you before you can get out of the way. It is uncertain whether the ball would have gone up the middle to score the winning run, or would have been a double-play ball. As it turns out, the ball ricochets into right field after hitting you. Is the ball still in play and does the Iowa Baseball Confederacy win this one, or is this a dead-ball play and will Swan have to hit again? It's your call.

9. Red Wilson is catching when the runner on first base breaks for second. Wilson goes into his throwing motion, but hits your mask as you were leaning in to get a close look at the pitch. Wilson's throw sails into center field and the runner goes on to third. Is this a throwing error on Wilson and are you in play, or should this be a dead ball when he was interfered with by you? What if Wilson had still thrown out the runner despite being interfered with by the umpire? It's your call.

10. Gonzalo Marquez takes off running from first base when Coca Gutierrez hits a screaming one-hopper right at the first baseman. Marquez assumes the first baseman will tag first base and then try to complete the double play at second base on him. Marquez decides to foil the plan by faking to go to second base and then retreating to first

base. Marquez outsmarts himself, however, as the first baseman's first play is to force him at second base. As the shortstop takes the throw he steps on second for the force and then throws to first to complete the double play. But the clueless Marquez is sliding back into first base, and gets hit with the ball in the back, allowing Gutierrez to beat the throw. Who's out and who's on? It's your call.

By now you should be either a veritable expert, or completely loony. Check the eighth inning answers.

EIGHTH INNING ANSWERS

1. Safe. Hofmann should have touched the plate while asking the umpire for an appeal. There are two ways to retire a runner who has missed a base—tag the runner or tag the missed base. Hofmann did neither. (Rule 7.10*b*—Any runner shall be called out, on appeal when with the ball in play, while advancing or returning to a base, he fails to touch each base in order before he or a missed base is tagged.) Going into the dugout does not affect the status of the runner—except after a dropped third strike (Rule 6.09*b*). This is not abandoning his effort to run—that only occurs between bases.

2. No run scores, this is still a force play. The force is not removed until a following runner is put out or the runner reaches the next base. (Rule 7.08*e*—He fails to reach the next base before a fielder tags him or the base, or in this case, he is called out for being out of the baseline, after he has been forced to advance by reason of the batter becoming a runner. Rule 7.12—If such third out is the result of a force play, neither preceding or following runners shall score. Rule 4.09*a*—*Exception:* A run is not scored if the runner advances to home base during a play in which the third out is made by any runner being forced out.)

3. The defense must appeal—the second baseman taking the throw on second may or may not be an appeal. If the umpire felt he was taking the throw as an unmistakable act of appeal, the umpire could recognize it. (Rule 7.10—An appeal should be clearly intended as an appeal, either by verbal request by the player or an act that unmistakably indicates an appeal to the umpire. A player inadvertently stepping on the base with ball in hand would not constitute an appeal. Rule 7.10*b*—Any runner shall be called out, on appeal when with the ball in play, while advancing or returning to a base, he fails to touch each base in order before he or a missed base is tagged.)

4. The run counts! This is not a force play, it is an appeal play at first base. A force play occurs when the batter becomes a runner (he did not—he was out on the fly ball). According to Rule 4.09b, all runners may score, if possible.

5. Yes, a pinch runner can be inserted because the ball is dead on the home run. If the ball was still alive, such as on a double, and he was off his base, no substitute would be allowed nor should the umpire call time. If tagged while off his base, Davis would be out. (Rule 3.03—A player or players may be substituted during a game at any time the ball is dead. Rule 5.10c—When an accident incapacitates a player or an umpire; if an accident to a runner is such as to prevent him from proceeding to a base to which he was entitled, as on a home run hit out of the playing field, or an award of one or more bases, a substitute runner shall be permitted to complete the play.)

6. Yes, it is a legal putout. This becomes a force play because the batter became a runner because of the dropped third strike, which caused all runners to be forced with the bases loaded. (See Rules 7.08e and 6.09b.) With less than two outs there would have been no force and the batter would have been out.

7. This is a judgment call by the umpire. After spectator interference, the umpire may do anything in good judgment to nullify the act. If the ump felt the runner would have scored he may allow him to do so, if not he can hold him at third base. (Rule 3.16—When there is spectator interference with any thrown or batted ball, the ball shall be dead at the moment of interference and the umpire shall impose such penalties as in his opinion will nullify the act of interference.)

8. The ball is dead the instant it hits the umpire. The batter is awarded first base and any runner forced to advance because of the batter's award does so. Since bases were loaded this forces in a run— the winning run—game over. (Rule 6.08d—The batter becomes a runner and is entitled to first base without liability to be put out when a fair ball touches an umpire or a runner in fair territory before touching a fielder. If a fair ball touches an umpire after having passed a fielder, other than the pitcher, or having touched a fielder, including the pitcher, the ball is in play.)

9. This is umpire's interference. Put the runner back to his original base (first) unless Wilson's throw retires him. If the throw results in an out, disregard the interference. (Rule 2.00—Umpire's interference occurs when an umpire hinders, impedes, or prevents a catcher's throw

attempting to prevent a stolen base. Rule 5.09b—The ball becomes dead and runners advance one base, or return to their bases, without liability to be put out when . . . the plate umpire interferes with the catcher's throw; runners may not advance. *Note:* The interference shall be disregarded if the catcher's throw retires the runner.)

10. Marquez is out at second, Gutierrez is safe at first. Marquez's unintentional interference was not illegal. (Rule 7.09f—If any batter or runner who has just been put out hinders or impedes any following play being made on a runner, such runner shall be declared out for the interference of his teammate—but the umpire must judge interference has occurred. If the batter or runner continues to advance—forward or backward to a base—after he has been put out, he shall not by that act alone be considered as confusing, hindering, or impeding the fielders.)

How are you doing? Hang in there and check those scores!

NINTH INNING

1. Jesus Vega at the plate. Two straight pitches on the outside corners, and you call them both strikes. Vega can't believe it. Vega steps out of the batter's box while he calls time and starts giving you the business in two or three languages. You listen to a little of the whining, but you soon get tired of it. When you tell Vega to get back in the box and hit, he refuses. You then tell the pitcher to pitch and he bounces a pitch about a foot in front of the plate. Is this pitch strike three or is the count now 1–2? It's your call.

2. You're working a two-man crew. With the bases loaded, Handsome Ransom Jackson doubles to right center field. All three runners score and Jackson tries for third on the throw home. You're the base umpire and you call Jackson out on the subsequent throw to third. The home plate umpire is calling Jackson safe at third at the same time. How do you resolve this mess?

3. In a tie game, Tobacco Chewin' Johnny Lanning has run the count full on the leadoff batter in the ninth inning. As Lanning begins to make his payoff pitch to the plate the ball slips out of his hand and dribbles about fifteen feet toward home plate. Is this ball four and do you give the batter a base on balls or call this no pitch and give Lanning another chance? It's your call.

4. Bases are loaded with Peninsula Pilots and Calvin "Nuke" LaLoosh lets go with a wild pitch. The Pilots begin to move up a base and when Durham Bulls catcher Crash Davis gets back to the screen to retrieve the ball he finds it lodged in the chain-link fence. Davis can't budge the ball from the screen and all three Peninsula runners circle the bases. Do you allow all the runners to score, or do you call a dead ball and let the runners advance only one base each? It's your call.

5. Bump Bailey is playing center field for the New York Knights. With two outs and the bases loaded he decides to make a hotdog catch in the outfield on a routine fly ball. Bailey tips his hat to the crowd and then proceeds to use his cap to catch the ball. Is this legal? If not, what is the call? It's your call.

6. The Mudville nine has runners on first and second base with no outs. Casey has come out of his slump and instead of striking out, he pops up to deep shortstop. You're umpiring the bases and you call an infield fly, but a gust of wind carries the ball out to short left field and the left fielder calls the shortstop off of the pop-up and attempts to make the catch himself. Does the infield fly rule still apply? It's your call.

7. Baltimore's do-everything player, Oyster Burns, is tiring in the ninth inning of a tie game. He is removed as the pitcher and moves to right field to bring in a lefthanded pitcher to face a lefthanded Altoona slugger. The Baltimore reliever strikes out the slugger for the second out. Altoona has a righthanded hitter coming up with a runner in scoring position, and a refreshed Burns wants to come back in to pitch. May Burns be moved back to the mound? It's your call.

8. A visiting National League team starts the game with a bang with eight straight hits. Five runs are in and the bases are loaded when the pitcher moves up to hit in the top of the first. The visiting team's manager decides he would like to play for a huge inning and wants to pinch-hit for his pitcher. Do you allow the substitution? It's your call.

9. Pittsburgh's Sure Shot Dunlap decides to pinch-hit Dandelion Fritz Pfeffer in place of Blimp Hayes in the bottom of the ninth of a tied game, but he forgets to tell the umpire about his substitution. Pfeffer steps in to the batter's box and drills the first pitch over the left field fence for the apparent game-winning homer. The Boston manager appeals to you that the pinch hitter batted out of order since he was never entered into the game. Is Pfeffer out or does this one belong to the Alleghenies? It's your call.

10. The Norfolk Tars trail by one run with one runner on and Yogi Berra batting. As usual in this book, there are two outs in the bottom of the ninth. Berra hits a pop-up behind first base. The first baseman goes back to make the play, but gets tangled up with a sportswriter who is on the field taking photographs. The ball falls harmlessly to the ground in foul territory. Is this interference? Is it a foul ball or is Berra out, or do you give the slugger another chance to win the game for the Tars? For the ninetieth and final time, it's your call.

Congratulations! Unless you're one of those people who skips around all over the place, you've now completed our arduous crash course in strange situations. The extraordinary now seems mundane, right? Well, turn to the ninth inning answers and let's find your final position on our umpiring ladder.

NINTH INNING ANSWERS

1. Strike three! (Rule 6.02c—If the batter refuses to take his position in the batter's box during his time at bat, the umpire shall order the pitcher to pitch, and shall call "strike" on each such pitch. The batter may take his proper position after any such pitch, and the regular ball and strike count shall continue, but if he does not take his proper position before three strikes are called, he shall be declared out.)

2. This is covered in the rulebook. Get all the players and managers away and decide which call is most likely correct. Be prepared to argue with the other manager. (Rule 9.04c—If different decisions should be made on one play by different umpires, the umpire-in-chief—in this case the plate umpire—shall call all the umpires into consultation, with no player or manager present. After consultation, the umpire-in-chief shall determine which decision shall prevail, based on which umpire was in best position and which decision was most likely correct. Play shall proceed as if only the final decision had been made.)

3. No pitch, give Lanning another chance. A pitch must cross the foul lines. (Rule 8.01d—A ball which slips out of a pitcher's hand and crosses the foul line shall be called a ball; otherwise it will be called no pitch. This would be a balk with men on base.)

4. The ball is dead any time it becomes lodged. Since it was a pitch the runners would get one base. (Rule 7.05h—Each runner including the batter-runner may, without liability to be put out, advance one base, if a ball, pitched to the batter, or thrown by the pitcher from his

position on the pitcher's plate to a base to catch a runner, goes into a stand or a bench, or over or through a field fence or backstop. The ball is dead.)

5. Bump messed up here. No catch. The batter and runners get three bases. That's right, a triple, and the batter may try for home at his own risk. (Rule 7.05*b*—Each runner including the batter-runner may, without liability to be put out advance three bases, if a fielder deliberately touches a fair ball with his cap, mask or any part of his uniform detached from its proper place on his person. The ball remains in play and the batter may advance to home base at his own peril.)

6. Yes, the infield fly rule is still in effect. (Rule 2.00—Pitcher, catcher and any outfielder who stations himself in the infield shall be considered an infielder for the purpose of this rule.)

7. Yes, Burns can come back to pitch, but only once during the same inning (Rule 3.03).

8. Do not allow the substitution, make the pitcher hit. (Rule 3.05*a*—The pitcher named in the batting order handed the umpire-in-chief as provided in Rule 4.01 shall pitch to the first batter until such batter is put out or reaches first base, unless the pitcher sustains injury.) Since the visitors haven't been in the field yet, the pitcher could not have pitched to the home team's first batter.

9. This one is over. The batter did not bat out of order because he was a substitute. Batting out of order occurs when a player already in the game bats in the improper spot. The fact that the manager failed to notify the umpire is covered under Rule 3.08*a*. (If no announcement of a substitution is made, the substitute shall be considered as having entered the game when, if a batter, he takes his place in the batter's box.)

10. If the interference is viewed by the umpire to be unintentional, the play stands. Call it a foul ball. If the interference is viewed by the umpire to be intentional, you could give Berra another chance. Or, if in your judgment, the fielder would have made the catch, you can call the batter out. (Rule 3.15—No person shall be allowed on the playing field during a game except players and coaches in uniform, managers, news photographers authorized by the home team, umpires, officers of the law in uniform and watchmen or other employees of the home club. In case of unintentional interference with play by any person herein authorized to be on the playing field . . . the ball is alive and in

play. If the interference is intentional, the ball shall be dead at the moment of the interference and the umpire shall impose such penalties as in his opinion will nullify the act of interference.) Fortunately, separate areas for working media are made available these days, and this situation rarely occurs.

Now that wasn't too hard was it? Better than final exams? Gum surgery?

That's it! You have completed your journey through our Hypothetical Horrors Zone. Check the promotion schedule to see how you did. Are you enshrined in Cooperstown, or are you ensconced in your La-Z Boy, commiserating with major league umpires you watch on TV?

Actually, this test was not designed to make a professional umpire out of you. They've got schools for that. Instead, we hoped to help you understand the proper calls in tough and weird situations.

Anybody can get the easy ones right. The umpires who can handle these situations are the umpires who can walk to their car after the game with their heads held high, not the umpires who need an escort to defend against an angry crowd.

UMPIRING PROMOTION SCHEDULE

83–90 POINTS: COOPERSTOWN

You are writing books, doing color commentary on television and they are clearing a spot for you next to Jocko Conlan and Bill Klem in the Hall of Fame.

75–82 POINTS: POST SEASON GLORY

You are umpiring in the League Championship Series and World Series games and are asked each year to lend your expertise in the All-Star Game.

67–74 POINTS: THE SHOW

You've made it to the majors. Now you get to argue and be verbally abused by the best.

59–66 POINTS: CLASS AAA

You're knocking on the door. You're also moving up in the world of travel. Check with the airlines and get a frequent-flyer program.

51–58 POINTS: CLASS AA
You've been transferred out of the Southern League but the trips are only slightly shorter. You're halfway home to the big leagues, but the fans are still pretty bush.

43–50 POINTS: SOUTHERN LEAGUE
This is Double-A baseball, of the most grueling variety. Trips of ten or more hours are common.

35–42 POINTS: CLASS A
No more trips to Gastonia, but you're still paying your dues and breaking out plenty of road maps.

27–34 POINTS: SOUTH ATLANTIC LEAGUE
See the world, from Charleston to Charleston. That's West Virginia to South Carolina. Otherwise known as a heck of a long drive. Welcome to the "low-A" leagues.

19–26 POINTS: ROOKIE LEAGUE
Half a season, with some fans, is better than no season at all.

11–18 POINTS: GULF COAST LEAGUE
Welcome to professional baseball. Almost. It's just like pro ball only different. You see, games are played at noon at deserted spring training complexes, and there are seldom any fans. Don't worry, though, the young and inexperienced players make up for that with their willingness to argue with the umpires.

3–10 POINTS: UMPIRING SCHOOL
Don't get stuck here and be a professional student.

0–2 POINTS: LA-Z BOY LEAGUE
Stay home and watch the game on television. You don't even know the rules well enough to deserve the opportunity to sit in the stands and yell at the umpires.